SDG-5

Gender Equality & Female Empowerment Policy for Sustainable Development

SDG-5

Gender Equality & Female Empowerment Policy for Sustainable Development

Edited by

Dr. Rubee Singh
Dr. Jacinta Dsilva
Dr. Kalpana Gopalan IAS

SDG-5 Gender Equality & Female Empowerment Policy for Sustainable Development

First Published 2021

ISBN 978-93-87537- 82-8

Published by:

CRESCENT PUBLISHING CORPORATION

4806/24, Mathur Lane,
Ansari Road, Darya Ganj,
New Delhi - 110 002
Ph.: 011 - 23244131
Mob.: + 91 - 9711991838, 9999021668
E-mail: crescentbook@gmail.com
Website: www.crescentpublishingcorp.weebly.com

Typesetting by
Priyanka Graphics
New Delhi

Printed at:
Roshan Offset Printers
Delhi

Printed in India

Contents

Acknowledgement

I would like to express my gratitude to the many people who saw me through this book; to all those who provided support, talked things over, read ,wrote, offered comments, allowed me to quote their remarks and assisted in the editing, proofreading and design.

The Omnipresent God, I very humbly thank to God for giving me the strength to edit this book and my coauthors **Dr. Jacinta Dsilva** and **Dr. Kalpana Gopalan IAS, Additional Chief Secretary**, Governtment of Karnataka, for her hardwork, dedication towards book.

I am also thankful to authorities of GLA University, as we are provided with all desired infrastructrure and motivation for research work.

I would like to thank **Mr. Shammi Bhutani (Founder & CEO of Crescent Publishing Corporation New Delhi)** and all staff member of publication house for enabling me to publish this book. Above all I want to thank my Parents, Teachers and Friends, who supported and encouraged me in spite of all the time it took me away from them. It was a long and difficult journey for them.

There are a few more educationists who contributed a lot in the form of their guidance, supervision and continuous support in carrying out my this book.

Special thanks to respected **Mr. Anil Swarup Sir (Ret. IAS Officer Former Secretary, School of Education, MHRD, Govt. of India, & Mr. Ram Charitra Sir, DIG CRP, Bhubaneswar** for giving me their valuable time in motivation, inspiration, and suggestion to edit this book.

Last and not the least: I beg forgiveness of all those who have been with me over the course of the years and whose names I could not mention because of scarcity of the place.

Prof. (Dr) Rubee Singh
Prof. (Dr) Jacinta Dsilva
Dr. Kalpana Gopalan IAS

Corresponding Address: Editor-in-Chief (Dr. Rubee Singh), Assistant Professor, Institute of Business Management, GLA University, Mathura (U.P.) India, Pin-281406, E-mai: rubee.singh@gla.ac.in

About the Author

Dr. Rubee Singh is an Editor, Author & Social Activist. She is an Assistant Professor of Human Resource in Department of Business Management, GLA University India. She has been awarded Honorary Doctorate in Human Rights & Peace from Royal American University USA in September 2019 for her outstanding contribution in social work. Recently awarded as Chartered Global Peace Building Professional (CGPP) for the academic year 2020-2021 by The George Washington University of Peace USA in May 2020

She holds a Doctorate in HR from Noida International University India, an MBA in HR from Dr. A.P.J Abdul Kalam Technical University India. She has presented papers in national and international conferences and published 10 books in which Unemployment in India, Management Principles & Practices published by Lambert Academic Publishing Germany, International Business Environment by Educreation Publishing India, Business Communication, Compensation Management, International Business Management, Legal Aspects of Business, Govt. Schemes for Child Protection in India by Pacific Book International India. More than 30 international & national papers/ articles include Scopus Elsevier SSRN, Thomson Reuters, Scientific Journals & National newspapers of India.

Dr Singh is a Managing Editor of 3 reputed Journals; IJIEMR, IJARSH & Management Senior, Research Advisor of IMRTC USA. Lifetime Senior Member of Asia Society for Researchers Hon Kong, ISRD U.K, Eurasia Group, TERA India, IARA India, AIDASCO Serbia, IRFSR Malaysia, Research Fora India, IMPARC India. She is editorial board members of many repute journal such as JAAR USA, Science PG Publishers USA, AJR Japan, IGI Global USA. She is a United Nations Volunteer and also a contributing author for Voices of Youth (UNICEF).

Invited by WEPS Forum of United Nations (UN Women) to attend IWD'20 in New York USA also invited by 'The Stem Women Project' Ghana to attend IWD20. She has received Certificate of Achievement from TalkLove Africa Foundation Nigeria for Women's Empowerment on IWD'20 & received TalkLove Africa Foundation Award in March 2020 for promoting Education Campaign in India. She is management advisor for Alokbortika Bangladesh. She is nominee for 'The Oscar for the World's Greatness Civility Humanitarians' Award 2020 London, She is Nominated by Asia Book of Records 2020 for World Records University United Kingdom for Honorary Doctorate in Records Breaking. Recently she is selected for 'National Youth Icon Award 2020" in GECL International award. Also selected and awarded as 'Top Most Beautiful Women' award 2020 by Talklove Africa Foundation Nigeria, Sanjeevani Seed of Knowledge Award 2020 by Sanjeevani World School Mumbai.

She received Linkedin Wonder Women award 19 & 20 by Linkedin on International Women's Day and COVID-19 Leadership Award by Sexy Brilliant Revolution Canada with unique objective to remove toxic words from organization. Her career success story has featured in eYS Magazine Autumn 2020, Sydney Australia. Dr Singh is accredited united nations faculty for women empowerment & gender equality. She is working on many global mission like women empowerment, gender equality, child education, poverty alleviation, child labor protection, child & girls trafficking etc, agenda 2030, She has ccompleted many certification course from United Nations on Social issues, Social Justice & SDG agenda 2030 & Health related courses from World Health Organization include COVID-19. She has completed one week certification course from UNICEF on child Protection - best management resource pack – how to plan, monitor & evaluate child protection programmes. She is an honorary life member of Women Economic Forum..

Also holds position of:

- National Secretary of IATM (Youth Wing) SInternational Anti Terrorism Movement India.
- Chairperson of NHRF- National Human Rights & Humanitarian Federation India for Delhi. State
- Volunteer member of International Human Rights Commission Europe & IHRO India.
- International and National Global Goodwill Ambassador in Peace and Human Rights include GGA USA, MBIMB Child Abuse Prevention Program UK.
- First International Supporter for Deadly Guardians Organization Australia at International level.
- Child Ambassador for India by Happy Ambassador Concept Finland
- International Goodwill Ambassador for Children's Rights, Canada
- Global Ambassador – India by African Youth Development Foundation
- National Record Holder (India Book of Records-2020) as Grand Master for Book Writing
- Selected as Grand Master by Asia Book of Records for International Business management Book in Asia Region for edition 2021
- National Ambassador of India for Reviewer Credits, Italy
- Senior Editor, Team Attorney Lex India.
- Great Warriors of Humanity by International Human Rights Advisory Council & All India Council of Human Rights, Liberties & Social Justice India

Dr. Singh has received two prestigious awards in the field of Research

- **'Young Scientist Award'20** by Elsevier Research Award at International Level in March 2020
- **Best Managing Editor Award** of the Year 19-20 by Elsevier SSRN for IJIEMR in Feb 2020

Dr Jacinta Dsilva

Dr Jacinta Dsilva, is an Assistant Professor in Marketing at Business Department, Modul University, Dubai as well as a Visiting Professor at Chongqing University, China and SP Jain School of Global Management Dubai. She has also worked at several other prestigious UAE Universities such as Emirates Aviation University, Higher Colleges of Technology and University of Wollongong in Dubai. She also worked as Lecturer at the prestigious St. Agnes College Mangalore, India for five years. She has pursued M. Com from Mumbai University and MBA from Karnataka State University. She was awarded PhD in Marketing from Coventry University, Coventry, UK for her work on 'Service quality in Low Cost Carrier' in 2017. She has been in teaching profession for 20 years and have gained immense respect from fellow faculty and students alike. Her areas of specialization are Marketing Management, Corporate Communication, Consumer Behavior, Service quality and Supply Chain Management.

Dr Dsilva has presented at several international conferences and has published at peer reviewed journals. At present, she is focusing on Ethics and Sustainability related subjects along with Corporate Communication. She is also involved in final thesis in undergraduate and graduate level students. She has also given valuable contribution in several places of work such accreditation academic advising and other career counselling related services. She has been a regular reviewer for popular journal such as the Journal of Hospitality and Tourism Management as well as International conferences organizations such as Research Synergy and Emerging Research Paradigms of Business and Social Sciences. Recently, she has also published a book called Business Communication, along with Dr Rubee Singh and has been collaborating with local and international researchers for future research work.

Dr. Kalpana Gopalan IAS

Dr.Kalpana Gopalan IAS is a composite public policy professional. A true versatilist, she wears many hats- practitioner, policy-maker, scholar, author, volunteer and mother. She secured the19thrank in the All India Combined Civil Service Examination, 1987. Her 33-year work experience in the Indian Administrative Service spans land administration, urban management, public distribution system, sports, rural development, youth, training and education. She is now the Additional Chief Secretary, Department of Youth Empowerment and Sports, Government of Karnataka.

Dr.Kalpana is recipient of the Mother Theresa Women Empowerment Award for "outstanding contribution to excellence in leadership", the International Human Rights Award under the Women of Courage category (2019) , the Sexy-Brilliant Covid Leadership Award and the Social Activist Pratibha Samman (2020). She was recognized as a "Great Warrior of Humanity" by the International Human Rights Advisory Council for her "outstanding performance, commitment, contribution and dedication towards the humanitarian services and best practices on COVID19 prevention" (2020); and was appreciated by UNICEF and the Rajiv Gandhi University of Health Sciences for support in Covid19 response (2020). She is a LinkedIn Wonder Woman and Inspirational Leader (2020). She was felicitated and awarded citations, commendations and appreciations by the Bangalore University, NITTE University, Yenepoya University, Mysore University, IJASRW (2020), Rajiv Gandhi University of Health Sciences, Visvesvarayya Institute of Technology, WeLEED-Empowering Women's Growth, Gulbarga University, Jain University, Ramaiah Institute of Technology, Acharya Institutions, Melkote Academy of Sanskrit, Sheshadripuram Trust, SJES Institutions (2019),Honorary Consul, Republic of Maldives (2015) and Institution of Engineers of India (2013). She stewarded the NLM-UNESCO 2000 award for Karnataka with her work in literacy and the Karnataka Ratna award 2013 for Cauvery Handicrafts. She is Advisor, Bangalore City Corporation; Honorary Consultant, Administrative Training Institute, Mysore; Member, Advisory Committee, Public Sector Advisory, Grant Thornton LLP; and Member Advisory Board, Government Blockchain Association India.

A hybrid leader with a unique mix of public service, business school and academic credentials, Kalpana combines a unique mix of academic and practical experience and works collaboratively across the private, public and not-for-profit sectors. She honed her research skills with a Doctorate and Masters in public policy from IIM Bangalore. She was rated among the "top two percent of doctoral candidates in the past decade" for her research on infrastructure public private partnerships. A gold medalist and university topper in her undergraduate and master's, she was Visiting Fellow at McGill and Concordia Universities in Canada; EU fellow in the University of Salerno in Italy; Chevening Gurukul scholar in the Institute of Development Studies, UK; and Maxwell Public Policy scholar in Syracuse University, USA. She trained in Evidence for Policy Design in the Centre for International Development, Harvard University, USA (2014), E-Governance strategy in the London School of Economics, UK (2017) and Advanced Women's Leadership in the Harris School of Public Policy, University of Chicago(2019). She was twice selected as a SA-YSSP scholar by the University of the Free State, Bloemfontein, South Africa and the International Institute for Applied Systems Analysis. She presents papers in national and international fora and has published three books and many journal articles. She is a sought-after speaker and has delivered over 250 talks on different aspects of public policy to national and global audiences.

Kalpana pursues her academic interests as Senior Research Fellow in the National Institute of Urban Affairs, New Delhi; Visiting Faculty/Fellow in the Institute of Social & Economic Change, Bangalore; Indian Institute of Science, Bangalore; Indian Institute of Management, Bangalore; Acharya Bangalore B-School; and Kuvempu Rural University, Shimoga. Member, Advisory Board, AIMS School of Business, Bangalore; Member,

Academic Council, Mahatma Gandhi Kashi Vidyapith, Varanasi; and Member, MDP Advisory Committee, Presidency University, Bangalore, India. She is Chief Editorial Advisor IJ360MR and Member, Editorial/Advisory Board of IJBST, IJASRW and IFERP journals.

Dr. Kalpana volunteers as Advisor, Akshayapatra Foundation, Bangalore; Chief Patron, NSS; Mentor, Asoka Innovators for the Public; Technical Advisor, Grassroots Research & Advocacy Movement, Mysore, India; Advisor, Bangalore Women Forum; Member, Advisory Panel, Centre for Health & Development, Mangalore; Speaker, HER Initiative, Maharashtra; Member of Advisory Board for World Congress on Women 2019 and member, YWCA. A prolific writer, blogger and speaker, she has served as Secretary, Toastmasters International (IIMB Orators). She has an active social media presence in LinkedIn, You Tube, Academia.edu and ssrn.com, Widely travelled in North America, Europe and Asia, Kalpana is comfortable living and working in a multi-cultural milieu. She relaxes to music, and in the company of her husband and two children.

About the Book

This ground-breaking collection of chapters includes the different behaviours, aspirations and needs of women and men. Gender equality also describes the absence of apparent or implied disparities among individuals based on gender, therefore, this book intends to highlight the disparity in the society even though we claim that there is equality. Government has instituted several laws and Acts in favour of women, but unfortunately, inspite of all the support by the constitutional and legal rights their freedom is still overlooked and a far reality. The female population in many countries till date are often exposed to discrimination, several kinds of mental and sexual harassment, moral discomfort and are still looked down upon. If we evaluate further, the living condition for females is worse in the rural areas and urban slums where they are exposed to all possible uncivilized behaviour from the male counterparts. The book highlights several reasons for such behaviour as lack of education, awareness of their rights. Some of the chapters underline the importance of paving the way for female empowerment with the help of law enforcement as well as increased awareness through education so that they can empower themselves.

In the twenty-first century, we need to create a synergy in our society which can only be evident if both genders work together to build it further. Female empowerment is commonly associated with social justice and equality, therefore, a critical topic to discuss in the unprecedented times when lockdown corporate senior management positions, which is notably higher than the global average (24 percent), but the percentage of women on corporate boards, that is in policy and decision making positions, is just 14 percent, and many of them are wives, sisters and mothers, which greatly dilutes their effectiveness. There are about 5000 IAS officers in India, of which a tiny fraction, 331, are women. It is a similar scenario among your fraternity. My son is a neurosurgery resident, and he has about 25 female colleagues scattered throughout the country. Oncology fares only slightly better, I presume.

At one level, the women's movement is about breaking barriers, overcoming limitations and challenging stereotypes. It comes easier to us, though. Urban, educated, English speaking; while our lives are not without struggles or hard work, the path is smoother; the doors open more readily for people like us. This is not true though, of people who are "not like us". So I want to transport you now to an arena that is very different from the India you and I know; to a *Bharat* ... where every change is a potential catastrophe, where every deviation from the accepted convention has to be negotiated *a priori*, and has consequences to be faced *a posteriori*. In *Bharat*, change happens incrementally, gradually, at times painfully. Those who negotiate that change, those who face those consequences, these are my real heroines and heroes. They break barriers and challenge stereotypes, but in doing so they create not waves, but ripples of accumulative, additive transformation.

Therefore, I speak of and for ordinary women, not celebrities or heroines. I speak of those who have transcended their personal circumstances, or adverse externalities, and carved out a future for themselves and those they love. I strongly believe that these individual stories together script the collective narrative of all women. In doing so, these ordinary stories of ordinary women, women like you and I, become a powerful, transformational and extraordinary narrative of women as a collective. Let me introduce some of them to you today.

For me, a stellar example of overcoming limitations is Sunidhi Manjunath. I met her at the Asha Kirana blind school in

Chikmagalur. All of 12 years old, she captivated me by her agility in blind chess. I said to her: "You will be a champion soon, Sunidhi". This was in January 2019. And she did it. In April 2019, she won the first prize in the first national open fide rating chess tournament. So my point is, we should expand our traditional understanding of employment n workplaces. Unusual choices like sports offer a platter of career choices which Sunidhi, for instance, has used to overcome her very obvious and serious handicap.

Let me narrate Mallika's story. She drives a buggy at the KLE Medical College Belgaum. Mallika lost her husband when she was very young, and had to bring up her two children, a boy and a girl, as a single mother. Luckily for Mallika, the women's wing of the KLE society took her under its wing. It is one example of how women can help women. She was trained to drive, provided employment,. and over a period of time she got her daughter married, educated her son, while she continues to drive. As Mallika told it to me, her story was a happy one. Looking at her with her bright cheery smile at 7 am in the morning, you would never guess the struggles she has had to overcome in life. For me, Mallika is a heroine.

Finally, let me take you on a flashback, some 35 odd years ago in Chennai. A young girl is pacing up and down her room, book in hand, preparing for her BA Final exams. But she has more than exams to worry her. She is facing her first serious confrontation with her parents. Always supportive, always emphasizing the importance of education, her parents quite unexpectedly catapulted to an officious uncle who was determined on getting her married. Naïve and nervous, not really knowing how to handle her situation, she just keeps insisting, or rather pleading: "I want to do my MA, I want to do in MA!" That was the extent of her horizon at that time, and MA degree was as far as she could dream. Anyways, it worked, and she did get to do her MA, and then joined the IAS, and then acquired two more Masters degrees, and then a PhD. And she did eventually marry too. That nineteen year old was me, and that rare instance of stubbornness defined the rest of my life thereafter.

This set me thinking. We speak of empowerment easily and often, we use the term loosely, as though it is an achievement. But what is empowerment really? The prefix "ëm" in em-power troubles me, as though it is something that the more powerful and privileged bestow upon the less powerful and privileged. Indeed, if you look at the dictionary or thesaurus, the synonyms jump out: Empower means "to *allow*", "to *give* power and authority".

That is not just condescending, it is not even true, is it? Look back to your own lives or other women that you know. When I look at people that I admire, whether women or men, no one gave them anything. They pulled themselves up by their bootstraps, not once or twice, but each time they fell or were pushed down. That includes me, I may look successful and fulfilled, but I was not handed anything in a platter. I have striven and coped and toiled. If anything, people around me made things more difficult, either deliberately or inadvertently. The so-called "empowered" women struggled, survived and thrived, over many years, slowly, gradually, at times painfully. Each story is different, but one thing is common, these women built their individual capability, and this made them not symbolic shells who were ***given*** power; but the true architects of their own self-empowerment.

Building Capability, that is the key! Building Capability, rather than empowerment, is a far more accurate description of my journey, and the journey of many women I know. If it sounds familiar, let me remind you, building capability is the underpinning of the Nobel Laureate Amartya Sen's Capability Approach. Sounds too theoretical? Well, let me make it simple. For me, this sums up my Capability Approach: "Don't give me a larger slice of the cake because I am a woman. What I want is not just a bite into your slice. I want to choose the cake I eat, its texture and flavor and colour, and I want to learn to bake it myself, and share it with you too, equally!"

The Capability Approach. What is the use of theory if it does not enable practice, help us live a better life? I spoke of the Nobel Laureate Amartya Sen's Capability Approach. Theory cannot remain an academic exercise, it has to be interpreted, translated and applied in our life and work. It is easier to remember and practice a concept when it is expressed in simple, everyday terms. If I give you a lecture on gender discrimination, it would display my scholarship. But you will not remember anything of value to take away, and, more importantly, to live by, and to practise.

The second reason is, while speaking of gender or other forms of discrimination, we speak of external factors. And it is true that social and structural issues play a large part in *creating* the problem. But the fact that the source of the problem lies outside us should not induce helplessness and inaction. You cannot wait till the world changes. You have to effect the change in yourself, impact your own life, and thereby become part of the solution. I believe that solutions to the intractable problems of the world are found, most of the time, by small gradual incremental choices of ordinary people like you and I. That is why I have not shown you pictures of a Gloria Steinem or Angela Davis. I have instead showcased three real women, their real stories.

Third, I believe that every problem has a solution, and that solution lies in simple but substantial action, not symbolism. It is not necessary to shout slogans and join marches; symbolic actions do have their value, but what will effect the substantial change are simple ordinary solutions practised with extraordinary diligence. Yes, just like Covid-19, hand-washing, distancing-simple solutions but substantial impact.

First, Seek and Search. Information, information, Information is key. Be a seeker and repository of knowledge. A woman entrepreneur has to familiarize herself with all the different opportunities, assistance, schemes, programs and institutions that are available to encourage women entrepreneurship. Generally, Indians as a whole, and Indian women in particular, tend to rely on family or friends or their cousin's sister in law for information. Well, there is no need to cut off the grape-wine, after all there is the great pleasure in human interaction. But as an entrepreneur, it is essential that you go above and beyond it. The internet is a great source of information, in fact the best and easiest of access. Scour government websites for information, not just the startup websites but different departmental websites of the central and state governments. For instance, Stand-Up India facilitates Bank loans upto 10 lakhs for women entrepreneurs. Trade Related Entrepreneurship Assistance and Development (TREAD)provides women with trade related training, information and counselling and grants of up to 30 percent of the total project cost. Karnataka has industrial policies specially tailored for women, in fact a whole chapter on women entrepreneurship. You should also familiarize yourself with local, national and global macro-economic trends, price fluctuations, inflation; economics may appear as a boring subject from outside, but once you get your teeth into it, it can be engrossing. I also notice in educated women a tendency to "skip" numbers, anything arithmetical, mathematical or even statistical; well, don't. Notice that I specifically said educated women; the vegetable vendor in Basavanagudi or the flowerseller in my neighbourhood temple are natural number crunchers.... And you should be too. So Seek, Search and Gather Information. That's the first ingredient in my recipe.

My second ingredient is Sharing. When we speak of women leading, in entrepreneurship as well as in other spheres of life and work, it is important that we capitalize on our strengths. One important strength we women have, our competitive advantage so to say, is Sisterhood. Don't confuse this with the water-cooler or locker room gossip of men. Our sisterhood goes beyond borders, there is an instant bond, a connection, between women regardless of where we come from or what language we speak. We must build on this, and definitely not let it be clouded by envy or backbiting. Everyone will have some black spots in their lives, some skeletons in their cupboards. How does it matter? Someone's husband has a girlfriend, someone's brother is a drunk, someone's daughter didn't get admission in Columbia...does it matter? We are professionals, we are women, let us help each other through our struggles and our strifes. If I can give one single reason for where I am today, it is by avoiding all negativity, all envy, all malice from my words and actions;

even when I am being hurt and harmed. Let me give you an example. Some years ago, I was working in an organization where I fell foul of my boss. His way of getting back at me was to isolate me completely, and deprive me of work entirely. My subordinates were instructed Not to submit any files or papers to me; and the entire organization, which was about 50000 strong, was Informally told not to approach me for any reason whatsoever. So much so that when one officer wished to invite me for his son's marriage, he met my husband and gave him the invitation. I was handling HR at the time, so you understand how untenable the situation became. How could I manage people that I could not meet? A cleaning lady used to come into my chamber every day. She was used to seeing me with lots and lots of work and always busy and in a hurry, and suddenly here I was, alone in my chamber, day after day, with no work and no people, but with a lot of time on my hands and an old rickety desktop computer for company. She hardly understood office politics, but she asked me one day: You are looking so bored, and more tired than when you were working late nights. Why don't you read something, why don't you write something? That was the trigger I needed. I sat and wrote a paper, a study of Bangalore city, its growth and its conflicts; and then I sent it off to an international conference. It got accepted, and I got an all-expenses paid trip to present the paper in a prestigious university in the UK. So my pointer to you is, share, nourish sisterhood, mentor other women, be a giver. You will grow along with your sisters.

My third proposition to you all is, be Socially Responsible. We tend to get caught up with our self, our life, our troubles. These things will always be there. There is only one way to overcome these, and that is by giving a hand to someone else. When I was administering the literacy program in the state, the Shaksharata Andollan, my most joyous moments came when I attended literacy groups of poor, underprivileged or tribal women. In the late evening after work, when they read out the alphabet or signed their name, their eyes shining with the light of accomplishment, it gave me a feeling of fulfillment that I will remember forever. Take up a cause, adopt a school, grow a tree, teach a child. Conduct your business not just efficiently, but ethically. Just as personal qualities of truth and positivity are important, so too social qualities such as environmental consciousness or a social conscience are important.

We are redefining our lives every day, in infinitesimally small ways. We do not always set out to break barriers or challenge stereotypes; we may simply seek what is right for us. And in doing so, we create change. Nothing is ever too trivial, everything is cumulatively creating a quiet revolution that is transforming our lives and transforming our ecosystem. I am sure that you will find in your own lives how you have contributed to a positive change. Today, let us together applaud our own contribution to that transformative revolution.

2

Opinions on Gender Equality in (Higher) Education and Science

Maria M. Uzelac1,[3] and Sanja J. Armakovic[2,3*]

1.Board Member of the Association for the International Development of Academic and Scientific Collaboration, Novi Sad, Republic of Serbia

2.Vice President of the Association for the International Development of Academic and Scientific Collaboration, Novi Sad, Republic of Serbia, *e-mail: sanja.armakovic@aidasco.org

3.University of Novi Sad, Faculty of Sciences, Department of Chemistry, Biochemistry and Environmental Protection, Novi Sad, Republic of Serbia

Abstract: In this article, we have discussed some specific topics related to the position of women in higher education and science in our country. Everybody agrees that these are challenging times and gender equality has never been more important. A lot of reports about gender equality and the position of women in different societies have been published over the years. However, specific aspects of women's position in higher education and scientific activities are rarely covered in detail. Developed societies are characterized by, at least, significant participation of female members, and these tend to achieve gender equality. Numerous measures have been implemented over the years to improve the position of women, however, not all parts of the world are equally developed concerning this topic. Achieving gender equality indeed demands enormous resources, however, the lack of financial resources must not be a justification for not doing anything. Women are facing additional challenges in the areas of higher education and science. The development of science and technology has changed the dynamics of our lives. The tremendous development of technology in all areas should have made our lives easier, however, the amount of work is constantly increasing and the work-family balance is seriously compromised. All of these facts make the position of women even more challenging. The purpose of this article is not just to mention some of those challenges, but also to promote and support the need for discussion on these important topics.

Keywords: Equality; Academy; Gender gaps

1. Introduction

All over the world, policymakers are dedicated to the improvement of educational and scientific activities in their countries. A good educational system provides access to necessary skills, enables the transfer of knowledge, and contributes to the creation of new young leaders.[1] On the other side, high-quality scientific activities provide development and sustainability.[2] There are no doubts that education and science are the barebones of society's development.[3]

While it has been evident that significant resources have been invested all over the world for the development of education and science, the problem of gender equality in these areas preserves. This topic is present for decades, however, certain parts of the world still haven't reached the necessary level. We are still facing the underrepresentation of women in these critical areas. Without doubts, gender equality is certainly one of the greatest challenges humanity ever had.[4]

Gender equality means a better and safer world for a living. Gender equality means harmony and brings different points of view. In countries with a high level of consciousness, gender equality is accepted as a normal state of society.[5] This means that in developed countries gender equality doesn't have to be artificially induced. Women there get executive roles according to their competence and achieve results. In such countries, women have equal (or close to equal) opportunities to work the same jobs as men, to earn the same amount of money for the same job as men, to have the same access to health and education, etc.[6]The number of such countries is not high, however, it is good that the problem of gender equality is recognized as a threat to the further development of humanity.[4,7]Many conventions and protocols have been established over the years[8], and it is certainly encouraging that Serbia has supported by ratification the Convention on the Elimination of All Forms of Discrimination against Women. On the road to the EU, Serbia has obliged to this and similar initiatives and, although the situation is improving, it is no secret that women should be much more present in government institutions at executive positions while preserving their true autonomy to make decisions independently.[9,10]

Several reports on gender equality in the case of Serbia have been made public over the last decade, and these reports provide important insights into the position of women in society. Some of the conclusions in such reports are that gender gaps in the work domain are particularly expressed and that women are less frequently employed in full-time equivalent jobs, in comparison to men. Such reports cover many relevant areas, but for this particular opportunity, we wanted to provide our understanding of the position of women in Serbia in the areas of education and science.

2. Education in Serbia

Aside from all possible challenges our country is facing in the last 30 years, people in Serbia, in general, have trust in the educational system. While the position of School and Teacher, from the institutional point of view, has been shaken in the last three decades, people in Serbia generally believe that education in public schools and Universities is the best possible choice for their children. The whole education is divided into four main stages (preschool, primary school, secondary school, and higher education) and each of these stages has specific positive and negative sides. Education in Serbia is free, while it should be noted that the number of students that can attend University for free is limited.

In 2003 Serbia officially signed the Bologna Process, triggering the tectonic changes of the Serbian education system, especially in the part dealing with higher education. While Bologna Process, in the beginning, reflected mainly to higher education, it produced a high influence on secondary education as well, which had to change to prepare future students for the faculties. Up to that point, the education system inherited from Yugoslavia was active, and a lot of people still believe that the old education system was better.

In general, the position of a teacher within any educational institution has been always treated with respect in Serbia. Unfortunately, the autonomy of elementary and high school teachers has decreased over the years, making sometimes challenging situations for teachers. This has also led to the fact that teaching positions at schools are not as popular as they used to be. This situation is also supported by the fact that the salary of the teacher in high school in Serbia equals around the national average salary.

In the last gender equality report of the National Agency for Statistics (NAS), dating from 2017 [12], it is stated for the year 2016 that 56 % of enrolled students are females and that 58 % of the graduated students are females. The same year was also characterize by the higher number of females (57%) who earned their Ph.D. Recently, the same agency reported that the female share in the total student population in 2019 is still higher. Officially, around 140 000 students are females, while around 109 000 students are males. When it comes to the area of natural sciences, the number of female students is even higher in comparison to the number of male students. These numbers are certainly encouraging, as they mean that future generations will produce more competent female leaders.

3. Women rectors in the Serbian academic community

The previous education system, that was active practically until 2005, was certainly characterized by the very small number of women present in the higher education at decision-making positions. On the other side, women were significantly present as teaching staff in primary and secondary schools. When it comes to the teaching staff of the preschool stage, it mainly consisted and still consists of women.

The share of women in education has also been commented on in the report published in 2016 by the Government of the Republic of Serbia [13]. In that document, it was stated that a much higher share of women is employed in sectors of education. Nevertheless, the same couldn't be stated for the share of women when it comes to decision making positions.

While many believe that the transition to the Bologna system could have been performed better in the case of Serbia, the authors of this text believe that it brought one very important novelty. Implementation of the Bologna Process certainly opened to Serbia the educational and scientific borders of the EU, and suddenly the exchange programs have become available. This was extremely important, especially taking into account the very difficult (and isolated) situation in the country until October 5th, 2000 [14]. Thanks to the Bologna Process, Serbian educational institutions got in contact with educational institutions all over Europe, where women were much more present as teaching staff, directors, deans, and parts of other important managerial bodies. This had a significant contribution to appointing women in Serbia at such crucial positions within institutions at all levels of education. Additionally, the opening of Serbia towards the EU also had benefits, in terms of possibilities for participation in large international projects. This opened numerous positions for women as well. Nowadays, the situation regarding the female teaching staff within public Universities in Serbia is improving. Anyhow, it could have been better, but it is improving.

Certainly, the most important executive academic position is rector. To illustrate the situation regarding the underrepresentation of women in the decision-making bodies of Universities in Serbia, we will focus on this topic in more detail. The largest, oldest, and the best ranked is certainly the University of Belgrade (UBG), followed by the University of Novi Sad (UNS), University of Niš (UNN), University of Kragujevac (UKG), etc. In the last few years, the first-mentioned has been steadily ranked in the famous Shanghai list as well. In its 115 years long history, the UBG had 42 rectors, of which only two were females. The current rector is female, and the previous female rector led UBG in the period from 2000 to 2004. The situation within the UNS is somewhat better. In its 60 years long history, it had 18 rectors and 3 of them were females, all in the last 25 years. UNN and UKG were never led by female rectors! It is certainly encouraging that in the last two decades there were female rectors at our two largest Universities, but at the same time, there is a lot of space for improvements.

4. Challenges for women in science

The development of international collaboration, ratification of important initiatives, participation in large projects, the assistance of the EU, are just some of the reasons thanks to which the number of women scientists in Serbia increased over the last two decades. However, it is necessary to make a distinction between the women scientists working on their Ph.D. and women scientists having a tenure-track position at some Faculty or Institute.

In general, an academic career depends on two components - scientific and teaching. To acquire a teaching position in higher education, it is necessary to meet the criteria in terms of performed scientific activities and published results. This is a critical component for women because research is very demanding from several aspects. Ph.D. studies and corresponding activities take several years and all these activities are happening in a critical period in terms of starting their own family. Very frequently, women postpone starting a family in order to finish the Ph.D. studies. Postdoc studies are also very frequent, which in the case of women means additional postpone of pregnancy.

According to the data of EUROSTAT [15] for the year 2018, women are having their first child at an older age in comparison to data for the year 2008. The numbers of EUROSTAT show that women in the EU are having their first child at 29. That number is slightly lower in the case of Serbia and is equal to 28. However, this number is much higher if only women working in science are taken into account. Although there is no data for this category, it is well known that women working in science very frequently have their first child long after their 30th birthday.

While Serbia has a very decent period for maternal leave (up to 12 paid months), pregnancy and absence from work bring additional challenges for women in science chasing a Ph.D. Aside from certain time-demanding administrative procedures, it is also challenging to cope with the scientific activities after a such long break. Ph.D. research is demanding itself and it usually needs to be carried in continuation. This is a huge challenge for women who wants to start a family and have a first child before their 30th birthday. It is not strange in Serbia that a certain amount of established professors consider pregnancy and maternal leave as a vacation for a woman! This contributes to decisions to postpone pregnancy after achieving a certain goal (e.g. full time teaching position in high school, tenure track or Ph.D. title at faculty, etc), so, as mentioned, it is not strange for women scientists in Serbia to give birth to a baby for the first time long after their 30th birthday.

Additionally, it is also important to mention the postdoc studies. Over the last two decades, this stage of professional improvement has become a must have in some regions. What makes the situation harder for women scientists is that this stage of a professional career can be even longer than the Ph.D. studies, bringing additional challenges for women to start a family and have a child.

5. Women in other decision-making roles

What is still concerning is the fact related to the important positions in education and science. In a previous chapter, we have mentioned the numbers related to the most powerful academic position (Rector of University). However, there are many more influencing positions, and this challenge is recognized as a serious task. According to EUROSTAT gender equality data [16], the percentage of positions held by women in senior management within the EU is still

not representative. For example, the percentage of female board members was less than 30% in 2019. However, that is a huge increase in comparison to the year 2004, when there was less than 10 % of female board members! What is even more important is that the percentage of female board members is steadily increasing over the years. With such an increase, gender equality with respect to this parameter within EU could be reached in 5-10 years.

Some countries have achieved outstanding results. For example, in 2019, Iceland and France had 45 % and 46 % of female board members, respectively. These countries were followed by Norway (40%), Italy (36%), UK (33%). It is also worthy of mentioning that Norway practically had all the time (in the 2004-2019 time interval) a significant percentage of female board members [17]. It is also important to mention that the law related to gender equality in selected countries significantly contributed to the increase in the presence of females in important boards.

There is no summarized data about the percentage of females in all board members in the case of Serbia, however National Agency for Statistics[18] in its document from 2017 reports that only 6.6 % of Municipal boards are led by females (mayor/president of the municipality), while 31.2% of Municipal board members are females. When it comes to the board directors, the lack of data is also evident, but in a study of Babovic [19] from 2014 (relying on the data from 2011), it is reported that the percentage of female board directors in companies in Serbia doesn't exceed 24%, depending on the region.

6. Importance of the proper model of behavior

When it comes to gender equality in higher education and science, besides laws and other instruments, it is very important to provide proper examples. The best way to promote some model of behavior is to act according to that model. In these regards, we would like to mention that certain institutions in Serbia might provide a little bit better examples.

For example, the Serbian Academy of Sciences and Arts (SASA). This renowned and probably the most prestigious academic institution in Serbia is a typical example of gender inequality since male academicians dominate. This is also recognized by the NAS, which states in its report for 2016 that more than 90% of all members are males. The section of SASA for Social sciences at that moment didn't have female members at all. Currently, the section of SASA for mathematics, physics and geosciences also doesn't have female members, out of 24 members! Not even in foreign members. Section of SASA for chemical and biochemical sciences has 3 female members, out of 23 members. The section of SASA for medical sciences has also 3 female members out of 25 members, while the section for historic sciences has 5 members out of 15. The art section of SASA has 2 female members out of 12 members.

The role of SASA and any national academy of sciences and arts, in the development of any society, is indisputable. Their members are highly qualified, accepted, and influential constituents of the academic community. It would be stronger than any law if important academic institutions would start to cherish gender diversity and promote a model in which both genders are adequately represented.

7. Conclusions

It is evident that the position of women is improving and the examples of actions within the EU surely confirm this statement. However, a lot of space for improvement in all areas is remaining. It is certainly necessary to continue with brave decisions and actions. To overcome the challenges related to gender equality, the whole society needs to be activated. Proper models of behavior have to be promoted and followed, and in these regards, special attention has to be focused on younger generations and future leaders. Therefore, gender equality has to be promoted in all aspects of education and science.

When we speak about challenges in front of humanity, frequently the first association is related to the enormous resources necessary to overcome those challenges. In situations when resources lack, a personal example is the best solution. Many people and institutions can contribute to the solution of gender equality simply by responsible decisions and by promoting personal examples. A lot of people agree that a personal example is stronger than any law.

Overcoming gender equality challenges and improving the position of women in science and education will require enormous dedication and resources. But, the outcome will be more rational humanity, which is one step closer to the world of harmony.

Acknowledgement

The authors are grateful to the members of AIDASCO for support and useful suggestions (www.aidasco.org).

References

1. Roser M, Nagdy M, Ortiz-Ospina E. Quality of Education. Our World In Data, 2013.

2. Niiniluoto I. Scientific Progress, The Stanford Encyclopedia of Philosophy. Winter Edition, Edward N. Zalta, 2019.

3. NavehEbrahim A, Karami V. A study of relationship between triple skills of department chairs and improvement of

educational quality. Quarterly Journal of Research and Planning in Higher Education. 2006, 39, 61–78.

4. Monroe K, Ozyurt S, Wrigley T, Alexander A. Gender equality in academia: Bad news from the trenches, and some possible solutions. Perspectives on Politics, 2008, 6(2), 215–233.

5. Williams C. Still a Man's World. University of California Press, Berkeley,1995.

6. Ceci, BSJ, Ginther, DK, Kahn S, Williams WM. Women in science: The path to progress, Scientific American Mind, 2015, 62–69.

7. Bailyn L. Breaking the Mold. Free Press, New York, 1993.

8. Frize M. More than just numbers: Report of the Canadian committee on women in engineering. University of New Brunswick, Canada, New Brunswick, 1992.

9. AkhavanKazemi M. Higher education and stable political development. Institute for Research and Planning in Higher Education, 2005, 1, 13–32.

10. Byrne EM. Women and science: The snark syndrome. Falmer Press, London, 1993.

11. Matyas ML. Obstacles and constraints on women in science: Preparation and participation in the scientific community. Women in science: A report from the field. London, In J.B. Kahle, Falmer Press, 1985.

12. http://www.mospi.gov.in/. 15 October, 2020.

13. http://socijalnoukljucivanje.gov.rs/en/new-gender-equality-index-for-the-republic-of-serbia-published/. 28 October, 2020.

14. Serbians overthrow Milosevic (Bulldozer Revolution), Global Nonviolent Action Database, Belgrade, 2000.

15. Official website of the EUROSTAT, https://ec.europa.eu/eurostat. 20 October, 2020.

16. https://ec.europa.eu/eurostat/web/sdi/gender-equality. 27 October, 2020.

17. Report onequalitybetween women and men in the EU, European Union, Luxembourg, 2019.

18. https://www.stat.gov.rs/sr-Latn/oblasti/stanovnistvo/statistika-polova, 25 October, 2020.

19. Baboviæ M, Polo•aj •ena u biznis sektoru u Srbiji studija, Ministry of Labour, Employment, Veteran and Social Policy, Belgrade, 2014.

3

Role of Women's Empowerment in Gender Equality and Human Rights in India

Dr. Rubee Singh [1]
Assistant Professor in HR,
Institute of Business Management,
GLA University, Mathura, India

Dr. Jacinta Dsilva[2]
Assistant Professor in Marketing
Department of Business Management
Modul University, Dubai

Dr. A. Arun Kumar[3]
Assistant Professor , Centre for Management Studies
ICFAI Law School
ICFAI Foundation for Higher education,
Hyderabad, India.

Abstract: This chapter focuses on a valid discussion on equity and equaligy among men and women. The chapter is based on a strong argument of the rights that are available to women and the ones that are implemented. The main aim of this chapter is to create awareness about the human rights provided to both the men and women as well to focus on the shortcomings of implementation even after so many years of independence. The chapter also intends to provide recommendation to improvise the human rights pertaining to women and work towards upliftment of the women particularly the workplaces irrespective of a woman works in a corporate office or is a rag picker.

Introduction

Gender equality between women and men refers to the equal rights, responsibilities and opportunities for women and men and girls and boys. Equality does not mean that women and men will become the same but that women's and men's rights, responsibilities and opportunities will not depend on whether they are born male or female. Gender equality implies that the interests, needs and priorities of both women and men are taken into consideration recognizing the diversity of different groups of women and men. Gender equity that provides a level playing field for men & women so that they have a fair chance to realize equal outcomes are a pre- condition for ensuring gender equality and human rights. The ultimate goal in gender equality is to ensure that women and men have equitable access to, and benefit from society's resources, opportunities and rewards. And, as part of this, women need to have equal participation in defining what is valued and how this can be achieved. Equity is a means. Equality is the result. Gender equity denotes an element of interpretation of social justice, usually based on tradition, custom, religion or culture, which is most often to the detriment to women. The Convention on the Elimination of All Forms of Discrimination against Women, also known as the Women's Bill of Rights, declares that countries should:

- Act to eliminate violations of women's rights, whether by private persons, groups or organizations,
- Endeavour to modify social and cultural patterns of conduct that stereotype either gender or put women in an inferior position,
- Ensure that women have equal rights in education and equal access to information,
- Eliminate discrimination against women in their access to health care,

- End discrimination against women in all matters relating to marriage and family relations.

The constitutional guarantees for Gender Equality and Human rights in India

For Indian citizens, the constitutional guarantees for empowerment of women are as follows: Fundamental Rights ensure empowerment of women thro'

Article 14- equal rights and opportunities for men and women in the political, economic and social sphere

Article 15- prohibition of discrimination on the grounds of sex, religion, caste etc

Article 15(3) - empowers the State to take affirmative measures for women

Article 16- provides for equality of opportunities in the matter of public appointments

The directive Principals ensure empowerment of women thro'

- Article 39- enjoins the state to provide an

– adequate means of livelihood to men and women and

– Equal pay for equal work

- Article 42- State to ensure the provision for just and humane condition of work and maternity relief.
- Article 51v (A) (e) - fundamental duty on every citizen to renounce the practices derogatory to the dignity of women.

Articulation of the demands and alternatives suggested by the women's movement constantly refer to the Fundamental Rights in the Constitution of India.

Women's Movement and Legal Reforms

When the government of India signed the **UN charter on Equality, Development and Peace** in 1975, the process of gender audit in the governance got an official stamp (Patel, 2002). In 1976, the Equal Remuneration Act was enacted to provide equal opportunities, equal treatment and equal wages for work of similar nature. Women's groups have been consistently doing public scrutiny of Maternity Benefit Act, 1961 and specific provisions for women in general labour laws, The Factories Act, 1948 - Section 34 provides that the State government can lay down rules prescribing weights that may be carried by men and women, The Contract Labour (Abolition and Regulation) Act and Rules- that separate provision of utilities for women and fixed working hours.

Though these laws have proper implementation mechanisms, there is no provision for monitoring the effect of these laws on women. Allowance for special provisions for women has often proven to be detrimental to their employment opportunities. Participation of workingwomen in the decision-making processes in the industrial and agrarian relations is abysmally low. Women's access to legal service largely remains inadequate in spite of the legal service Act, 1987.[1]

The Labour Laws for Empowerment of Women

The labour laws for empowerment of women are based on principle of gender justice. They are as follows:

- Equal Remuneration Act, 1976 ensures equal opportunity, equal treatment and equal wages.
- Maternity Benefit Act, 1961 provides 90 days paid leave for working women
- The Factories Act, 1948 - Section 34 provides that the State government can lay down rules prescribing weights that may be carried by men and women.
- The Contract Labour (Abolition and Regulation) Act and Rules- separate provision of utilities for women and fixed working hours.
- Women in the unorganized sector don't get benefits of the labour laws in spite

UNORGANISED WORKERS' *SOCIAL SECURITY. ACT*, *2008*. N0. 33 OF *2008*.

In the formal or organized sector, there are industrial legislations and other protective legislations for workers. Most of these legislative provisions, unfortunately, seem to be working against the interests of workers, lack implementation and need reform. Government regulated minimum wages ensure only the bare essentials of survival but even that basic level is denied to workers in the informal sector. Factory inspectors usually avoid reporting as employers complain of low profitability, threaten closure and bribe them to keep quiet. At present crèches are provided in industries that employ more than 30 women employees and there too, ways and means are used to avoid this facility by the employers. There is no provision for providing crèches in the service sector and for both men and women working in shifts.[2]

In India, The Equal Remuneration Act, 1976 was enacted pursuant to Article 39 (d) of the Constitution of India provides for the payment of equal remuneration to men and women workers, for providing equal opportunities to women and men and for the prevention of discrimination on the grounds of sex against women in the matter of employment. The task of ensuring that there is no discrimination is very difficult, as there is no effective way of implementing the limited findings of the advisory committee. Secondly the definition and evaluation of the same work or work of similar nature leave much to be desired. Even the courts have used different expressions relating to valuation of identical work. This is one of the least invoked legislation.

Maternity Benefit Act, 1961 provides for maternity benefit in case of childbirth, miscarriages, abortions, Medical Termination of Pregnancies (Maps) and tubectomy. Establishments employing less than ten persons are left out from the purview of the Maternity Benefit Act or the Employees State Insurance Act. Under the present Maternity Benefit Act, 1961 the eligibility for maternity leave is that the woman before availing the leave must have worked for eighty days in that establishment or organization. These eighty days include paid holidays and weekly holidays and the period for which she was laid off. In many organizations they are never allowed to complete the required number of days on record.

Women Movement is demanding an umbrella legislation to cover all women (From formal/ organised as well as informal/ unorganised sectors of the economy) under maternity protection and ratification of ILO Convention No. 183.

Violation of basic Human Rights in Informal Sector

The informal sector as opposed to the formal sector is often loosely defined as one in which workers do not have recognition as workers and work without any social protection. In the informal sector, women workers are forced to work without contracts, without social security, with low wages under bad working conditions. In the absence of health insurance, income security, it is difficult for women workers in informal sector to place importance on their health. The lack of income security often has direct consequence on the access to education for the children of women workers in informal sector. They are not able to study and alleviate their poverty. Often children get absorbed into the informal sector themselves as adults due to lack of education or as children to help adults earn more (e.g. home based workers, vendors, self employed)[3] Unorganised labour is usually perceived as 'poor' and as a beneficiary, consequently there are provisions in the national budgets to help them out of their poverty and vulnerability. They are treated as beneficiaries of anti-poverty programs. The main concern of informal sector workers is irregular employment (Patel & Karne, 2006).

Rag pickers- Poorest of the Poor

A Case Study of Women Rag Pickers in Mumbai[4] has revealed that urbanization and the use of land for large-scale agriculture have led to mass migrations to the cities, where the displaced rural poor eke out a living on the margins of India's over-crowded cities. Unable to find work in the formal sector, many turn to street trading and rubbish collection in order to survive. Rag picking is a caste and gender based activity. Rag pickers comprise the poorest of the poor – an estimated 25,000 of them in Mumbai, dwelling in shanties, mainly women and children who collect garbage - plastic, paper, metal, etc., usually from municipal dustbins, landfills and garbage dumps for recycling. They work seven days a week, earning on average less than Rs. 60 / 70 a day. They help maintain the environment of Mumbai by keeping the streets clean and recycling and re-using waste. Mumbai produces 6000 metric tons (600 truckloads) of garbage every day, of which around 7 to 8% is collected by rag pickers. Rag pickers are highly vulnerable because they have few assets and few alternative livelihood options. Because of their hazardous working conditions the rag pickers suffer many more illnesses and injuries than the general population. Rag pickers live in constant fear of displacement, while others simply sleep on the pavements. Illiteracy among rag pickers and their children is high, and access to formal training or employment is non-existent. Many rag pickers have limited knowledge of their rights as citizens, including basic rights like access to free primary education.

No skills training

Women are not taught specific skills and are themselves diffident to take up skill training. The government's existing ITI network has a low number of women students. There is a need for improvement of courses and optimal use of space and teachers.

Abuse in Special Economic Zones

Adoption of Export oriented model and competition for foreign investment has led to the opening of more and more Special Economic Zones (also Free Trade Zones and Export Processing Zones etc.). In these zones labour laws are generally not applicable. Women are being used as 'cheap labour' force. They work under harsh working conditions. There is the abuse of labour and human rights and several instances of sexual harassment at workplace. Governments have had tendency to turn a blind eye to the abuse by capitalists to keep foreign investment.

Night Work- the Issue and the debate

Business process outsourcing has resulted into thousands of call centers employing young, computer savvy, English-knowing women for night work.

Global tourism industry has given rise to mushrooming of bars and night clubs throughout Asia. In Mumbai, bar girls campaigned to work at night, as their work is possible only during that time and also more remunerative. Due to pressure of women elected representatives of local self government bodies, bar dancing is now banned in Maharashtra.

According to ILO, 'night signifies a time period of 'at least 11 consecutive hours, including an interval between 10 p.m. and 7 a.m.[5] But many women workers face a lot of problems due to work at night including sexual harassment, molestation and rape. It is unfair to put a blanket prohibition on night work is discrimination against women to prevent access to jobs and contravening the principle of equality. The questions regarding sexual harassment and assault on them needs to be addressed.

The state and employers must be forced to provide safe work environment and safe transport to women employees.

Sexual harassment at Workplace

Accusations of sexual harassment are much more common today, reflecting the new consciousness and a new sense of power of people to end inappropriate behavior directed towards them. The existence of an effective, informal conflict resolution process is immensely important.

To address Sexual harassment in the informal and small-scale industries, free trade zones, special economic zones; the labour departments may be directed to set up complaints committees and give them publicity or it could be made mandatory for every industrial estate and export zone to have its governing body set up a grievance cell for complaints (Sujatha, 2007).

This will require co-operation between women's groups, official bodies, trade unions and employers. Women's groups can play an active role in disseminating information about sexual harassment and redressal procedures in industrial zones and estates. They can also raise the issue of the definition of skills and equal pay for comparable work so as to tackle gender inequality at the workplace. The Sexual Harassment at Workplace (Prevention) Act must be enacted by the nation states to provide a remedy within the criminal justice system. This is to provide for prevention of sexual harassment of women and women an employee that is work related (Ghadially, 2007).

Need for a Policy for Women's Employment

A policy for women's employment has to include strategies for challenging the sexual division of labour and gender ideology inside as well as outside the workplace.

Policies for access- include access to employment, education, training, credit etc.

- Policies to improve the quality of employment, including her position in the household.
- Policies to preserve employment and to protect material and human resources and assets.

Proper Implementation of Laws and Schemes for Working Women

1. The existing labour legislation, i.e. the Industrial Disputes Act, the Factories Act, the E.S.I.S. Act and the Minimum Wages Act, should not be withdrawn but strengthened to cover all workers.
2. Some mechanism is required to evaluate the value of work under ERA.
3. Minimum wages need to be strictly implemented with ward level committees of workers.

4. Employment Guarantee Scheme-The central and state government has to ensure macro policies that will absorb workers in labour intensive units and occupations. The Employment Guarantee Scheme needs to be expanded and improved for

urban workers. The focus of such employment schemes can be on building infrastructure, slum development and housing. The National Renewal Fund should be extended to cover the unorganised sector and a substantial part should go into the retraining of workers.

Law Reform

Crèches should be provided for children of all workers and not merely women workers irrespective of the number of employees. There could be a common fund for each industry.

Family Leave: The minimum paid maternity leave period to be applicable to ALL working mothers irrespective of the necessary length of continuous service or the number of employees, irrespective whether married or un married and whether the child is natural born or adopted. Birth or adoptive fathers of a new child entitled to paid paternity leave on the birth or adoption of a child Employees to have a right to take time off to care for children, disabled or sick dependants. The options available include: unpaid leave with automatic re-entry to an equivalent post in terms of grade, type of work etc., Part time working, Temporary re-arrangement of working pattern, Flexi-time Request Right available to working parents with young children (below 5 years of age or employees who have to care for disabled or sick dependants. The request can cover: the employee will have a right to return to work following availing of any of the above leave. The staff member must undertake in writing to return to work. No employee will suffer a detriment, be unfairly dismissed or be discriminated against for a reason connected, with pregnancy, childbirth, maternity, paternity, adoption, dependent care leave or the right to request flexible working, or time off to take care for a dependant. There shall be no loss of seniority, sick leave entitlements and incremental progression

Legal Protection for Informal Sector

Legal protection has to be given to the informal sector worker in the form of regular employment, notice period, compensatory pay or some form of unemployment insurance. It has been a long- standing demand of the representatives of the informal sector workers, trade unions and NGOs (Non Governmental Organisations) that workers should be registered as daily or piece rated workers with an identity card. This single act would provide information on the number of irregular workers and access to them for welfare measures. Social welfare for the informal sector workers can be implemented by levying a cess on employers in industrial estates. Social services can be dispensed to the workers through existing government infrastructure and tripartite boards.

Rag-pickers' need

Recognition as workers, Supplementary development programs, Vocational training for skill up gradation, Provision for maternity benefit and post natal medical facilities, Protection against domestic violence and sexual harassment, Family benefits, Medical reimbursements, Retirement benefits (old age pension), Insurance schemes and policies, Compulsory savings schemes, Micro finance schemes and interest free loans, Legal guidance and awareness (Patel and Karne, 2006).

Problems in Implementation of Mahatma Gandhi National Rural Employment Guarantee

Scheme under MGNAREGA:

The Mahatma Gandhi National Rural Employment Guarantee Act aims at enhancing the livelihood security of people in rural areas by guaranteeing hundred days of wage-employment in a financial year to a rural household whose adult members volunteer to do unskilled manual work. Poor women from all over the country are seeking and getting employment under this scheme.

1. Though wages are apparently equal between men and women what happens is the allocation of work is different- men do trench digging which carries more wages. Women have been saying they can also do this work without trouble. Secondly wages are often paid

to the group of a few from the same village on the basis of equal pay for men and women but the group leader determines how much a woman gets. This should be remedied.

2. The most serious complaint is lack of facilities- shelter; schooling for the children of women who are the major reporters for EGS work.

3. The most serious lacunae are the stopping of registration of applicants. This has made it difficult to know how many need work. The work site merely records how many turn up. The absence of registering how many want (not just turn up) with details of who the applicants are again loses data regarding the status of the worker- small farmer, marginal farmer, landless worker etc; details of land holding. Plans will be better done if one knows the status of the worker also with regard to improving agriculture.

4. The timing of EGS work is another problem. It clashes with seasonal migration.

5. The most important demand of women workers on EGS sites is skill up-gradation. They are tired of unskilled manual labour and building roads. The objective of employment under EGS is building good infrastructure. But it is done so badly the asset does not last even one year. This needs to be rectified. More choices and better technologies should be introduced in EGS work. Labour processes and labour relations in EGS work should be humanised and gender- sensitive. Women employees working for the scheme should not be targeted for population control programmes.

Emphasis on Education and Skills

A clear emphasis needs to be given to education, type of education of poor and especially of women. Women's access to employment is limited (amongst other reasons) because of lack of education and skills. The central and state government has a free education policy for girls but there is no follow up on the number of dropouts. Girls usually drop out from the high school. Special attention and incentives should be given to girls and parents for them to return to school.

Capacity Building and Training

Extra allocations of funds will be necessary for tying up the training institutions with job placement organisations or industries. Trainings for jobs have to be combined with additional inputs around

building other life-skills towards critical awareness about women's status, improvement in negotiating skills and programs around building and maintaining women's assets including savings.

Social Audits

International consumer and workers groups have attempted social audits at the firm level to ensure workers' rights. They have to be made mandatory not only for export firms but for all production units.

Self Help Group Movement

Self Help Groups are organisations of women from the downtrodden section of the society that empower the women to be self reliant through capacity and confidence building and by making micro-credit available and accessible to women. The SHG movement has taught women the value of saving and the strength of working as a group.

Recommendations for strengthening the SHGs:

- Groups should be only formed by NGOs or Women Development Corporations with the requisite knowledge and ethos of SHG development and micro-credit movement.
- Once an NGO is selected, the nurturing grants should be released every quarter to it, after reviewing training

milestones, group savings and internal lending data and not on the basis of bank gradation. NGOs should receive nurturing grants for at least five years, during which they should support the group.

- A state level agency should be appointed to train NGOs and also be permitted to appoint their own NGOs to implement the programme in addition to implementation through its field workers.
- SHG groups are not broken up by the banks insistence to drop the member who is a defaulter or whose family member is a defaulter of the bank.
- Along with initiatives improving the programme delivery mechanism, bankers need to be trained and sensitized every three months, because of the high turnover of bankers in rural areas and the ignorance of bankers coming from urban postings to the needs of rural areas.
- NGO releases should not be made contingent to the group taking up economic activities. NGOs should be evaluated in the basis of group capacity building and training.
- This SHG movement is now at the crossroads and is poised for expansion and the problems need to be addressed immediately.

Property and Land Rights

There is much gender bias in our property laws. Everything appears equal on paper and that is where it ends (Patel, 2009).

Recommendations

- Testamentary powers that deny the daughters their property rights should be restricted
- Allow daughters full right of residence in the parental dwelling houses.

- Women must be given 'the right to residence' hence putting private household property in the joint names of partners. A care however has to be taken that wherever women have property in their name, men did not appropriate under the pretext of property being in joint name.

A woman on being abused in her matrimonial home has little choice but to continue to endure it. Her natal household is usually unwilling to have her back for fear of the social stigma attached to single women. These and other considerations restrict a women's reliance on her parents' households in times of potentially dangerous marital relations. **Bill on Matrimonial property** has been drafted that needs to be passed. The matrimonial property bill will give her rights

The 73rd and 74th Amendments to the Constitution

The 73rd and 74th Amendments to the Constitution providing for 33% reservations of seats for women in Panchayats and Municipalities as of now we have 1.2 million women elected representatives in gram *panchayat, taluka panchayat, zilla panchayat,* municipal councils and municipal corporations (Patel, 2002). The Recent amendments in Bihar and Maharashtra have ensured 50% reservation for women in local self government bodies. UNDP Report, 2001 reported, "The evidence on gender and decentralisation in India suggests that while women have played a positive role in addressing, or attempting to address, a range of practical gender needs (Practical gender needs Practical Gender Needs are identified keeping into consideration, gender based division of labour or women's subordinate position in the economy. They are a response to immediate perceived necessity, identified within a specific context. They are practical in nature and often are concerned with inadequacies in living conditions such as provision of fuel, water, healthcare and employment.), their impact on strategic gender needs (Strategic gender needs Strategic Gender Needs are different in different economic contexts and are determined by statutory provisions, affirmative action by the state, pro-active role of the employers to enhance women's position in the economy and social movements) is not remarkable." (UNDP 2001). Following the introduction of economic liberalization policies in 1991, India has registered steady gains in terms of conventional economic indices such as external trade, investment inflows, and foreign exchange reserves. However, globalization has also caused the feminization of poverty.

To counter this trend of marginalization of women, it is necessary to address the gender imbalance in decision-making positions. A Constitutional Amendment Bill seeking 33 percent reservation for women in parliament and state legislatures has, however, been scuttled by three successive governments since 1996, even while each party swears by its commitment to gender equity.

The reasons for this curious schism showcase a classic example of gender-class-caste alignments and divisions, under political compulsions. This paper examines this ongoing gender-caste-class imbroglio, in the context of Indian affirmative action policies (economic, social, political), which have generated "backlash" reactions.

Countering Violence against Women

Violence against women (VAW) is a manifestation of historically unequal power relations between men and women, which have led to domination over and discrimination against women by men and to the prevention of the full advancement of women. VAW is one of the crucial social mechanisms by which women are forced into a subordinate position compared with men. VAW constitutes a violation of the rights and fundamental freedoms of women and impairs or nullifies their enjoyment of those rights and freedoms. VAW is an obstacle to the achievement of equality, development and peace, as recognized in the Nairobi Forward-looking Strategies for the Advancement of Women in 1985, in which a set of measures to combat violence against women was recommended. Definition of gender based violence: VAW prevents the full implementation of the UN Convention on the Elimination of All Forms of Discrimination against Women (CEDAW), a landmark international agreement that affirms principles of fundamental human rights and equality for women and girls initiated by the UN and adopted by the member countries. According CEDAW, the term gender-based violence "GBV" includes actual or threatened physical, sexual and psychological violence occurring in the family or community.VAW is understood as

I. Physical, sexual and psychological violence occurring in the family, including battering, sexual abuse of female children in the household, dowry-related violence, marital rape, widow burning, female infanticide, pre-birth elimination of girls, crimes against women and girls in the name of honour, female genital mutilation and other traditional practices harmful to women, non-spousal violence and violence related to exploitation;

II. Physical, sexual and psychological violence occurring within the general community, including rape, sexual abuse, sexual harassment and intimidation at work, in educational institutions and elsewhere, trafficking in women and forced prostitution;

III. Physical, sexual and psychological violence perpetrated or condoned by the State, wherever it occurs.

Under the Indian Penal Code (IPC), the following sections are applied in cases of VAW:

IPC Section	Nature of Offence
304 B	Dowry death/ murder
354	Criminal assault of women to outrage women's modesty
366	Kidnap, abduction and marriage of a women by force.
366 A	Procurement of a minor girl
366 B	Import of girl from a foreign country

374	Rape
376 A	Intercourse by a man with his wife during judicial separation
376 B	Intercourse by a public servant with woman in his custody
376 C	Intercourse by superintendent of jail, remand home with women in his custody.
376 D	Intercourse by any member of the management or staff of a hospital with any womanin that hospital
498 A	Husband or in-laws subjecting a woman to cruelty
509	Word, gesture or act intended to insult the modesty of a woman

The PCPNDT Act, 2002:

Adverse child sex ratio due to pre birth elimination of girls has posed a major threat to survival of girls and women in India (Patel, 2010). In this context strict implementation of Pre-conception and Prenatal Diagnostic Techniques (Regulation and Prevention of Misuse) Act (2002) is mandatory. PNDT Act was enacted in 1994 by the Centre followed by similar Acts by several state governments and union territories of India during 1988 (after Maharahstra legislation to regulate prenatal sex determination tests), as a result of pressure created by Forum Against Sex-determination and Sex –pre selection. But there was a gross violation of this central legislation.

In response to the public interest petition filed by Dr. Sabu George, Centre for Inquiry into Health and Allied Themes Mumbai) and MASUM fought on their behalf by the Lawyers Collective (Delhi)[6]; the Supreme Court of India gave a directive on 4-5-2001 to all state governments to make an effective and prompt implementation of the Pre-natal Diagnostics Techniques (Regulation and Prevention of Misuse) Act (enacted in 1994 and brought into operation from 1-1-1996). Now, it stands renamed as "The Pre-conception and Pre-natal Diagnostic Techniques (Prohibition of Sex Selection) Act".

Recently enacted Prenatal Diagnostic Techniques (Prohibition of Sex Selection) Act, 2003 tightens the screws on sex selection at pre-conception stage and puts in place a string of checks and balance to ensure that the act is effective.[7]

The Pre-natal Diagnostics Techniques

(Regulation and Prevention of Misuse) Amendment Act, 2002 received the assent of the President of India on 17-1-2003. The Act provides "for the prohibition of sex selection, before or after conception, and for regulation of pre-natal diagnostic techniques for the purposes of detecting genetic abnormalities or metabolic disorders or sex-linked disorders and for the prevention of their misuse for sex determination leading to female foeticide and for matters connected therewith or incidental thereto".

Under the Act, the person who seeks help for sex selection can face, at first conviction, imprisonment for a 3-year period and be required to pay a fine of Rs. 50000. The state Medical Council can suspend the registration of the doctor involved in such malpractice and, at the stage of conviction, can remove his/her name from the register of the council.

The Pre-Natal Diagnostic Techniques (Regulation and Prevention of Misuse) Amendment Rules, 2003 have activated the implementation machinery to curb nefarious practices contributing for MISSING GIRLS. According to the rules this all bodies under PNDT Act namely Genetic Counseling Centre, Genetic Laboratories or Genetic Clinic cannot function unless registered.[8]

The Bombay Municipal Corporation has initiated a drive against the unauthorised determination of gender of the foetus as per the directive of the Ministry of Law and Justice. All sonography centres are required to register themselves with the appropriate authority- the medical officer of the particular ward. The registration certificate and the message that under no circumstances, sex of foetus will be disclosed are mandatory to be displayed.[9]

The Shortcomings of the PNDT Act (2003) lie in criteria set for establishing a genetic counseling centre, genetic laboratory and genetic clinic/ultrasound clinic/imaging centre and person qualified to perform the tests.

- The terms genetic clinic/ultrasound clinic/imaging centre can't be used interchangeably.

But the Act does.

- Moreover, the amended Act should have categorically defined persons, laboratories, hospitals, institutions involved in pre-conception sex-selective techniques such as artificial reproductive techniques and pre-implantation genetic diagnosis.
- Who is a qualified medical geneticist? As per the Act, " a person who possesses a degree or diploma or certificate in medical genetics in the field of PNDT or has minimum 2 years experience after obtaining any medical qualification under the MCI Act 1956 or a P.G. in biological sciences". Many medical experts feel that a degree or diploma or 2 years experience in medical genetics can't be made synonymous.[10]
- As per the Act, an ultrasound machine falls under the requirement of genetic clinic, while it is widely used also by the hospitals and nursing homes not conducting Pre-implantation Genetic Diagnosis (PGD) and PNDT.

Ban on the Advertisements of SD & SP Techniques:

Another important initiative that has been taken is against any institution or agency whose advertisement or displayed promotional poster or television serial is suggestive of any inviting gestures involving/supporting sex determination. MASUM, Pune made a complain to the Maharashtra State Women's Commission against Balaji Telefilms because its top rated television serial's episode telecast during February 2002 showed a young couple checking the sex of their unborn baby. The Commission approached Bombay Municipal Corporation (BMC) and a First Investigation Report (FIR) was lodged at the police station. After an uproar created by the Commission, the Balaji tele-film came forward to salvage the damage by preparing an ad based on the Commission's script that conveyed that sex determination tests for selective abortion of female foetus is a criminal offence. Now there is another battle brewing. The women's groups insist that the ad should be telecast for 3 months before each episode, while the Balaji Tele-films found it too much.[1]

The Protection of Women from Domestic Violence, 2005

An Act to provide for more effective protection of the rights of women guaranteed under the Constitution who are victims of violence of any kind occurring within the family and for matters connected therewith or incidental thereto. The bill on domestic Violence circulated in 2002 had generated heated debate around the issue, whether casual/ occasional beating should be considered as "domestic violence". [12] After massive signature campaign and lobbying, the Indian women managed to get THE PROTECTION OF WOMEN FROM DOMESTIC VIOLENCE Act, 2005 to provide for more effective protection of the rights of women guaranteed under the Constitution who are victims of violence-physical (beating, slapping, hitting, kicking, pushing), sexual (forced intercourse, forcing her to look at pornography or any other obscene pictures or material and child sexual abuse), verbal (name-calling and insults), psychological- and economic (preventing one's wife from taking up a job or forcing her to leave job) and emotional abuse of any kind occurring within the family. Domestic violence under the act includes harassment by way of unlawful dowry demands to the women or her relatives. It empowers the women victim to stay in the matrimonial, shared household and/or parental home whether or not she has nay title in the household. Recently formulated rules of the Act also empower the protection officer, police, public hospital and the community to take proactive steps to stop the violence and provide services to the victim.

The scope of this legislation has been widened to include persons who have "shared households and are related by consanguinity, marriage or a relationship in the nature of marriage or adoption to relationship with family members-— Even those women who are sisters, widows, mothers, single women or living with the abuser entitled to get protection."

As a result of the pressure of women's groups, health activists and judicial activism, new legal provisions such as recognition of the right to residence of a woman in the parental or matrimonial homes, provision for the appointment of protection officers and the recognition of service providers, gender sensitisation trainings for Protection Officers and Judges with regard to criminal legal system-substantive law, procedural law, rules and infrastructure and budgetary allocation for strengthening the structures and mechanisms for implementation of laws have been provided (Jesani, 2011).

Current Concerns on Sexual Violence Against Women

The Criminal Law (Amendment) Bill, 2013 was passed by the Lok Sabha on 19th March, 2013 and by the Rajya Sabha on 21st March, 2013. The President of India has accorded his assent to the Bill on 2nd April, 2013 and it is now called the Criminal Law (Amendment) Act, 2013

Thousands of individuals and groups made online submissions asking for a comprehensive law that prohibits sexual violence, while ensuring an efficient criminal justice system. There is a broad understanding that any such law should focus on more than just penetrating sexual assault, as proposed in the *Criminal Law Amendment Act, 2013*. It is imperative that the definition of sexual assault is broad enough to include anal, oral and digital rape, as well as rape with objects, marital rape and sexual assault against transgender people. Judicious implementation of Protection of Children from Sexual Offense Act, 2012 is demanded by citizens' fora, women's groups and child rights organisations. After 30 years of consistent effort, Indian women have managed to get The Sexual Harassment of Women at Workplace (Prevention, Prohibition and Redressal)

Act, 2013 and rules for the same are awaited so that the Act can be implemented.

Need for Legal Education

There is a need to provide public education through electronic media, community radio, seminars and public meetings on the following laws having direct bearing on women.

(1)	(2)
Ministry of Women and Child Development	
1	The Commission of Sati (Prevention) Act, 1987
2	Dowry Prohibition Act, 1961
3	Indecent Representation of Women (Prohibition) Act, 1986
4	Immoral Traffic (Prevention) Act, 1956
5	**Protection of Women from Domestic Violence Act, 2005**
6	National Commission for Women Act, 1990
7	The Prohibition of Child Marriage Act, 2006
8	Juvenile Justice (Care and Protection of Children) Act, 2000
Ministry of Labour & Employment	
9	Bonded Labour System (Abolition) Act, 1976
10	Contract Labour (Regulation & Abolition) Act, 1979
List of Acts having direct bearing on women	
11	Employees State Insurance Act, 1948
12	Equal Remuneration Act, 1976
13	Factories Act, 1948
14	Inter-state Migrant Workmen (Regulation of Employment & Conditions ofService) Act, 1979
15	Legal Practitioners (Women) Act, 1923
16	Maternity Benefit Act, 1961
17	Minimum Wages Act, 1948

18	Child Labour (Prohibition and Regulation) Act, 1986
19	Payment of Wages Act, 1936
20	Plantations Labour Act, 1951
21	Workmen's Compensation Act, 1923
22	Beedi & Cigar Workers (Conditions of Employment) Act, 1966
23	Cine Workers and Cinema Theatre Workers (Regulation of Employment) Act, 1981
Legislative Department	
24	Foreign Marriage Act, 1969
25	Guardians and Wards Act. 1890
26	Indian Succession Act, 1925
27	Married Women's Property Act, 1874
28	Hindu Marriage Act, 1955
29	Hindu Succession Act, 1956
30	Indian Divorce Act, 1869
31	Hindu Minority & Guardianship Act, 1956
32	Hindu Adoption & Maintenance Act, 1956
33	Special Marriage Act, 1954
34	Muslim Personal Law (Shariat) Application Act, 1937
35	Relevant provisions of Indian Evidence Act
36	Converts Marriage Dissolution Act, 1966
37	Christian Marriage Act, 1872
Ministry of Health & Family Welfare	
38	Medical Termination of Pregnancy Act, 1971
39	Pre-natal Diagnostic Techniques (Regulation & Prevention of Misuse) Act,1994
40	Mental Health Act, 1987

Ministry of Home Affairs	
41	Relevant provisions of Indian Penal Code, 1860
42	Relevant provisions of Code of Criminal Procedure
Department of Justice	
43	Family Courts Act, 1984
Department of Mines	
44	Mines Act, 1952

Source: Ministry of Women & child Development, Government of India 2008.

Conclusion

There is a need for an affirmative action to protect girls, young and elderly women from discrimination and violence, at the same time to establish their human rights. It must address the following areas of intervention.

1. **Improve Women's Economic Capacities**: Improve women's access to and control of income and assets, recognize her shared right to the family home, and incorporate the principle of division of community property in divorce laws. Productive assets and property are critical to strengthening the economic and social status of women, providing income opportunities and improved respect for women outside marriage and family.

2. **Strengthen and expand Training and sensitization Programs**: Programme designed to train, sensitize and inter-link those working at critical entry points to identify and treat abused women should be a priority, with one aim being increased accountability across institutions. Such programmes should be tailored for medical personnel, the judiciary, counseling and other support service providers.

3. **Dilaasa** model of one stop crisis centre housed in the public hospital to facilitate collective intervention of medical staff,

police and NGO must be replicated throughout the country.

4. **Effective use of the Media to build Public Awareness**: Mobilisation of communities around campaigns such as that for "Zero Tolerance of Violence" requires improved skills and capacity among NGOs to enter new forms of dialogue with journalists and media personnel to heighten awareness of human rights and their significance for addressing domestic violence.

5. **Programmes designed for the batterers**: must be introduced in both the state and voluntary sectors. In order to promote a holistic approach to prevention as well as intervention, the deficiency in programmes designed for men needs to be addressed.

6. **Addressing VAW through Education**: Prevention of domestic violence ultimately depends upon changing the norms of society regarding violence as means of conflict resolution and traditional attitudes about gender. To achieve this, there must be introduction of gender and human rights in the curricula of schools, universities, professional colleges, and other training colleges. Along with this, there must be recognition and commitment to the principle of free compulsory primary and secondary education for girls.

The Indian state has been pro-active so far as legal safeguards for women are concerned. The provision of protection of women is key intervention in the Twelfth Five Year Plan. Ministry of Women and Child Development has launched public education on laws concerning women. It has set out proactive, affirmative approaches and actions necessary for realizing the rights of women and providing equality of opportunity. Involvement of civil society groups, women's groups, educational institutions and judicial activism can strengthen these efforts.

References

Ghadially, Rehana (2007) Urban Women in Contemporary India: A Reader, Delhi: Sage Publications.

Jesani, Amar (2011) "*Violence* Against Women: Health and Health *Care* Issues Review of

Selected Indian Works", *www.scribd.com › Research › Health & Medicine, May, 8.*

Kumar Uday. K, Sowmyya. T, Kumar, A. A. (2014), Women Empowerment in Rural India with the help of Various Programmes, ZENITH International Journal of Multidisciplinary Research, 4(7), 91-98.

Patel Vibhuti (2002) *Women's Challenges of the New Millennium*, Delhi: Gyan Publications. Patel, Vibhuti and Manisha Karne (Ed.) (2006) *The Macro Economic Policies and the Millennium Development Goals*, Delhi: Gyan Publications.

Patel, Vibhuti (Ed.) (2009) *Discourse on Women and Empowerment*, Delhi: The Woman Press. Patel, Vibhuti (Ed.) (2010) *Girls and Girlhoods at Threshold of Youth and Gender*, Delhi: The Woman Press.

Sujatha, D. (2007) *Discrimination at Workplace: A Critical Study*, Hyderabad: ICFAI University.

UNDP (2001), *Decentralisation in India- Challenges and Opportunities*, United Nations development programme, New Delhi.

4

Empowering Women to Discover Purpose, Succeed & Grow

Dr. Hazel Herrington

Founder & CEO- Destiny Arise, Australia
Global Goodwill Ambassador

Starting and succeeding in business is a journey, we were all born with a purpose as we entered this world tiny, innocent and helpless, yet everything we have to reach our fullness in this world is impacted and encoded in our DNA. To discover your purpose as a successful entrepreneur, you must know who you are, where you are, when you are to act, and how you are to act. This will help you to map out your mind, spirit, and soul to be aligned with the vision for your business.

I've come across and read about several game-changers, as you probably have too. If you watch them closely they all possess one thing in common and this is true regardless of their reach and impact. The truth is they all started out just like the rest of us – as ordinary people. But they never stopped there like the rest of us rather they nurtured their leadership skills in them to stand out tall among the crowd.

What made them remarkable leaders what was their remarkable drive and passion to make a difference in their fields. Enthusiasm, coupled with an aspired "reach" and a "vision" that was bigger than 'normal'. Do you want to discover your purpose and change the world with your leadership skills?

Here are 5 ways to discover your purpose, succeed and grow in business.

1. HAVE SELF-CONFIDENCE

Lots of individuals are battling with identity crisis and have tried to create a public image for themselves by imitating celebrities and sports stars. Many have even undergone expensive and dangerous plastic surgeries just to look like their favorite stars. This is as a result of low self-esteem and personality crisis. Self-confidence and satisfaction in life depend on much more than looking good. True happiness comes from discovering and fulfilling your life's purpose. While growing up a vast majority of us have imbibed a negative notion about life, feeling we are unlovable, not-good-at-this-or that, feeling we are a lost cause. Success in life is not defined by how you look or what you have achieved in life but purpose. Know your worth and be sure of your self and what you are capable of, in business self-confidence allows you to be fearless and to confront challenges or criticism that may come your way.

2. CONTINUE TO DEVELOP YOUR SKILLS

Continue to develop your personal skills, knowledge, wisdom, and understanding of your purpose. If you need education, certifications, licensing, affiliations and/or associations, mentorship, life coaching, etc. in order to be successful start one day at a time. Research your avenues and set goals to achieve them. Schedule at least one day, and one hour of the week to accomplish the tasks toward developing and accomplishing your vision.

3. TAKE RISKS

Have the courage to take risks without knowing whether you will succeed or not. Planning and continuing to plan will help you to remain aligned to your vision, most entrepreneurs fail in one year of their startup due to improper planning, lack of persistence and a quitting mentality, in order to fully implement your vision be willing to take risks, dream big, see the future beyond the natural. Looking at all of the obstacles that you are facing and consider as limitations. Make a list of what is factual and what you think or thought to be a limitation. SEEK WISDOM from Mentors and Business Coaches. Most things that we think are limitations can be proven to not be limitations. A courageous leader is prepared to take risks when no one else will and raises difficult issues, is ready to give difficult feedback, and share unpopular opinions.

4. GAIN SELF-AWARENESS

In order to discover your purpose as an entrepreneur you need to spend time gaining SELF-AWARENESS. Most visionaries are successfully aligned with their vision because they know their own strengths and weaknesses. As a leader this will give you a better understanding of your own unique abilities and help you to work on building an authentic version of yourself. The greatest fulfillment and joy come from being your true authentic self and increase your own credibility. Many people are not aware that they are created awesome and can achieve far more than their self-limiting beliefs have hindered them from attaining. A vast majority settle for less than what they are capable of achieving.

5. OVERCOME FEAR

Many people would love to stop working a boring, possibly low-paying, nine to five job, and instead launch their own business, where they are their own boss based off their own passions and vision. But they don't because it means leaving their comfort zone and risking failure. This is quite understandable, but if you want change you can't just keep doing the same old things. Once I realized that truth and acted on it, said "NO!" to fear of taking action my entire life turned around. Yours can too.

How do you develop your leadership skillset and discover your purpose? Where do you even start? Dr. Hazel Herrington will help you create your own, tailored, high performance path. OR, support others in finding and tailoring theirs!

Dr.Hazel Herrington (Honorary)

Australia Humanitarian Global Goodwill Ambassador, Founding Director Destiny Arise, Multiple Award Winning Entrepreneur, Business Consultant, Global Keynote Speaker.

- **Pan African Thrive Legend Award Honoree/USA.**
- **World Greatness Award Honoree/ UK.**
- **Global Impact Award for Entrepreneurship and Community Building Honoree / Zimbabwe.**
- **2020 Australia Woman of the year nominee.**
- **Australia Top 100 Women of Influence by Australian Financial Review Nominee.**
- **AusMumpreneur multi-cultural award nominee.**

Are you looking to be a changer maker you can contact Dr. Hazel Herrington @ email: hazel@hazelherrington.com and you can find more details about her through **www. meethazelherrington.com**

5

Understanding Women's Issues through the Lens of Media

Dr. Hina Kausar
Assistant Professor, GLA University, Mathura

Anupama Gupta
Research Scholar, Jamia Millia Islamia, New Delhi

Introduction

Women are the wealth of India and they have contributed in almost every field and made country feel proud at every occasion. They are in front, leading the country, making mile stones and source of inspiration for many. In the 21st century India is fast emerging as a global power but for half of its population, the women's struggle to live life with dignity continues. Women empowerment in India is still a distant dream. There still exists a wide gap between the goals enunciated in the constitution, legislation, policies, plans, programs and related mechanisms on the one hand and the situational reality of the status of women in India, on the other hand.[1]

Media has proved to be one of the important instruments of social change in Indian society. In the corridors of the social change institutions, it is observed that media promotes consumer tastes and values, often alien to Indian culture and traditions. Today media is not playing the role of the Fourth Estate as a watchdog of democracy but there is too much commercialisation and sensationalism involving violence, sex, portrayal of women which is indecent and objectionable. It tends to reduce the legitimate space for treatment of gender issues concerns which is vital for the development and empowerment of women in the society.

Women Empowerment in India

The most significant and longest social movement continuing is movement for emancipation of women. Though the primary goal for women empowerment is to improve the quality of life of women but it has also deep ramifications in social, economic and political scenario of body polity. The media through its reach to people at large has been instrumental though not to the extent desired in supporting the movement for women emancipation by focusing neglect and marginalization of the position of the women in society.

Although discrimination against and exploitation of women are global phenomena, their consequences are more tragic in the some parts of the globe particularly in under developed countries where, ignorance, deprivation of the basic necessities of life, and the ever-growing pressure of transition from tradition to modernity- all combine to aggravate the inequalities that women suffer to a point at which their existence is reduced to a continuous battle for survival. Improving the status of women is regarded as the key to narrowing the gender gap and achieving a better quality of life.

The soaring crime rates and violence against women in the country reflects women as weaker sex who are being dominated and exploited. They face violence inside and outside the family throughout their lives. The mass media needs to focus on the health, crimes against women, wage discrimination, gender inequality, declining sex ratio, under-representation of women in important positions etc. The various scheme incorporated by the govt. requires wider coverage so that women especially from economically weaker section can be benefitted from them.

Role of Media

Media is the mirror of society and media reports are reflection of happenings in the society. Media has immense power to influence the masses and Information and Communication Technologies (ICT) has further revolutionised its significance Media has an important role to play – to create awakening in women to achieve their potential as the prime movers of change in society. In today's world, print and electronic media play a vital role in effectively conveying message that needs to be conveyed. Media, which wields immense power in a democracy - a power which is only expanding and not diminishing, needs carrying out a focused attention about women- related issues and the portrayal of women. It is, perhaps, necessary that the stabilizing force of women must be brought home to the Indian people. In every family and society, there is an ethical and spiritual space, which has been traditionally dominated by women. The media can play a salutary and a liberating role to give to the women the distinctive and the exclusive space, which must belong to them to enable them to generate the ethical and moralizing impulses for the entire society.

Constitutional and Legal Provisions Relating To Obscenity and Indecent Representation of Women

It is observed that in recent time media is representing women in an indecent way. Media has emerged as a major exploiter of women. It is seen to flout all norms relating to obscenity, decency and morality. There is a systematic overdose of nudity and vulgarity. In the media industry, women are treated as goods to promote sales. We cannot be mute spectators to the indecent representation of women. It is our duty to take cognizance of the activities that destroy the very foundation of Indian society and its culture.

The Indian Constitution in its Preamble, Fundamental Rights, Fundamental Duties and Directive Principles not only grants equality to women, but also empowers the State to adopt measures of positive discrimination in favour of women. Within the framework of a democratic polity, our laws, development policies, plans and programmes have aimed at women's advancement in different spheres. India has also ratified various international conventions and human rights instruments committing to secure equal rights of women. Key among them are Universal Declaration of Human Rights (UDHR), Millennium Development Goals (MDGs)[2] and Convention on Elimination of All Forms of Discrimination Against Women (CEDAW) in 1993.

The Indian Penal Code in Section 292, 293, and 294 IPC mentions laws to curb obscenity. The terms obscenity, indecent, or vulgar are difficult to define, as they are intricately linked to the moral value in a society. The test of obscenity is whether the tendency of the matter, charged with obscenity, is to deprave and corrupt those whose minds are open to such immoral influences and into whose hands a publication of this sort may fall. Obscenity deal with sale, hire, distribution, public exhibition, circulation, import, export or advertisement, etc. of any matter which is obscene. What is important is the need to protect society against the potential harm that may flow from obscene material and to ensure respect for freedom of expression which needs to be balanced with free flow of information.[3]

In spite of all these provisions, there is growing indecent representation of women or references to women publications, particularly in advertisements which have the effect of denigrating women and are derogatory to women. Though there may be no specific intentions of these advertisements, publications, etc to have an effect of depraving or corrupting persons. Therefore the **Indecent Representation of Women (Prohibition) Act 1986** was legislated to effectively prohibit indecent representation of women through any publication, media or advertisement. The object of this Act is to prevent depiction of the figure, form of body of women in any indecent form which is likely to deprave, corrupt, and injure the public morality or morals. The Indecent Representation of Women (Prohibition) Act, 1986 provides for the regulation of representation of women in the media. It prohibits indecent representation of women through advertisements, books, writings, paintings, figures or in any other manner. Section 4 prohibits the production, sale, hire, distribution, circulation, sending by post any books, pamphlets, slide, film, writing, drawing, painting etc., which contain indecent representation of women in any form. Yet advertisements showing women in an indecent way are aired day in and day out and hardly any action is taken. The National Commission of Women (NCW) has suggested modifications in the Act and elaborates upon ways to strengthen it and make it workable so that the objectives can be achieved.[4]

The Constitution of India guarantees equality to women and also provides special provisions which empowers the State to adopt measures of positive discrimination in favour of women for neutralizing the cumulative socio economic, education and political disadvantages faced by them. Fundamental Rights, among others, ensure equality before the law and equal protection of law; prohibits discrimination against any citizen on grounds of religion, race, caste, sex or place of birth, and guarantee equality of opportunity to all citizens in matters relating to employment. Articles 14, 15, 15(3), 16, 39(a), 39(b), 39(c) and 42 of the Constitution are of specific importance in this regard.

(i) Equality before law. **(Article 14)**

(ii) The State not to discriminate against any citizen on grounds only of religion, race, caste, **sex**, place of birth or any of them **(Article 15 (i))**

(iii) The State to make any special provision in favour of women and children **(Article 15(3))**

(iv) Equality of opportunity for all citizens in matters relating to public employment **(Article 16)**

(v) The State to direct its policy towards securing for men and **women** equally the right to an adequate means of livelihood **(Article 39(a));** and equal pay for equal work for both men and **women (Article 39(d))**

(vi) To promote justice, on a basis of equal opportunity and to provide free legal aid by suitable legislation or scheme or in any other way to ensure that opportunities for securing justice are not denied to any citizen by reason of economic or other disabilities **(Article 39 A)**

(vii) The State to make provision for securing just and humane conditions of work and for maternity relief**(Article 42)**

(viii) The State to promote with special care the educational and economic interests of the weaker sections of the people and to protect them from social injustice and all forms of exploitation **(Article 46)**

(ix) The State to raise the level of nutrition and the standard of living of its people **(Article 47)**

(x) To promote harmony and the spirit of common brotherhood amongst all the people of India and to renounce practices derogatory to the dignity of **women (Article 51(A) (e))**

Section 67 of **The Information Technology Act, 2000** is the most serious legislative measure against pornography. The wordings of section 67 are wide enough to cover all perpetrators of cyber pornography, be it the Internet service providers, web hosting entities or the persons behind the actual website. The Act prescribes imprisonment of either description for a term which may extend to 5 years and with fine which may extend to Rs. 1 lakh in the case of first conviction and in the event of a second or subsequent conviction with imprisonment of either description for a term which may extend to 10 years and also with fine which may extend to Rs. 2 lakh.[5]

Media Coverage of Women Issues

By and large the media scene in India is that media does not address serious issues about exploitation and unequal treatment to women in different spheres but is keen in reporting sex related incidents by way of sensationalizing news of atrocities on women. Thus instead of highlighting the exploitation of woman they end up becoming one of the reasons in increase of violence as their coverage more often than not tend to glorify the crime against women. It is true that media has brought to light, as never before, certain misdemeanours against women but in a very subtle manner it also perpetuated the stereotyped image of woman as a householder and an inconsequential entity in the traditional value system. Generally, women's problems never figure on the front page of a newspaper unless it is a gruesome murder or a case of rape. Newspapers even on women's page does not usually address relevant issues for women empowerment but reporting is concerned with beauty tips recipes, fashion syndrome etc.

It is unfortunate that there is lack of sensitivity among the newspapers in general to women and their problems. In this regard, a Study was conducted by the Media Advocacy Group viz. "Violence against Women: Media Coverage and Representation". The Media Advocacy Group made the following recommendations on reporting violence against the women.

(i) Media needs to take an extended, broader view of crimes against women. It has to be instrumental in conducting a social audit on factors responsible for increasing crimes, particularly against women and children, including indifferent investigative procedures, miscarriage of justice, and growing social impunity of the perpetrators of crime.

(ii) It also has to be instrumental in creating an awareness among civil society of the causes and nature of the crime itself, and of the preventive measures.

(iii) When treating these issues, media has to be extremely factual and empirical. The study also stated that the only regulation that governs a sensitive reporting on this issue is that the rape victim's name should not be disclosed. Barring this, the study found that everything else is graphically reported. Often the victim's family name and address is cited, making a mockery in the letter and spirit of the regulation. Though much of this violation and malpractice are committed by a small group of publications, others are spurred on to imitate and keep pace with the sensational trend.

Therefore, self-regulation and self-monitoring with extreme care and caution is very much required on the part of media. Aarushi murder case is another prime example of irresponsible and sensational reporting by the Media. The gruesome murder of a teenage girl for days have been the sound basis of increased TRPs of the News Channels. The media both electronic and print are morally and legally bound to avoid sensationalisation of news relating to victims of crimes. The Press Council of India had already drawn guidelines on the subject and appeals to media to follow them meticulously while reporting atrocities on women/child.

Limited coverage in Media Newspapers cover women's problems drawing the attention of policymakers to issues requiring immediate attention such as the adverse sex ratio, infant and maternal mortality, crime against women and the effects of poverty on women and their families. But this coverage is very limited with the rest of the space occupied by cinema actresses, models, video jockeys (veejays) and the rich women and their hobbies. Many of the women's magazines are devoted to fashion, glamour, beauty aids, weight reduction, cookery and how to sharpen 'feminine instincts' to keep men and their in-laws happy. There are comparatively fewer articles on career opportunities, health awareness, entrepreneurship, legal aid, counselling services, childcare services and financial management.

This portrayal of women in media has led the National Commission for Women to recommend amendment in the Indecent Representation of Women (Prohibition Act), 1986. The NCW wants to include new technologies like MMS and the electronic media and some which were left outside the ambit of the Act like posters and TV serials which perpetuate stereotypes of women.

The distortion of realities by the media has increased the gap of understanding between the different sections of society. Effective informative communication is one of the most important channels for the growth and development of women in the informal or unorganized sector, as without information regarding services and benefits available through legislation, government schemes, banks and voluntary organizations, women can hardly take advantage of them.

Thus the media should take into consideration the following points.

(i) The media must project the working women in the unorganized sector as worker and not merely as performing the duties of wife/daughter. They being major earners, they must be projected as producers and not merely consumers.

(ii) The media should make deliberate attempts to not only project the problems of women in poverty, but should monitor in such a way that conflicting role models are not depicted, nor derogatory references to their work are made.

(iii) To improve content and coverage, coordinated efforts for increased interaction between NGO's, women's social action group, research organizations, institutes of mass communication, and the media personnel should be developed.

Women Journalist in Media

In such a rapidly changing environment, women in media have a large responsibility in not only changing attitude towards women but also shaping public opinion. With women holding responsible position in newspapers or electronic media, their competency should extend to a wider area and a range of issues. More importantly, a woman journalist is expected to show more sensitivity to issues relating to women and to more meaningful insights and perspectives. Like most professions, in the media too, women have struck out boldly, beating a path, which is both impressive and inspiring. The last five years have seen them pouring out into the mainstream, acquiring hitherto unattainable positions and proving their mettle, be it the print or the television media. In short, women have become indispensable in the field. Women's organizations and media groups must play an active role in promoting this change. It is heartening that a wide variety of women's media initiatives are making a positive impact.

The rough estimates however show that although the number of women in both the media has increased in absolute terms, their ratio to men has more or less remained static. A deliberate policy for ensuring adequate representation of women both in the public and private sectors of the media is therefore a must, not only for giving women a source of livelihood but also to ensure their adequate and effective representation, and to make the media truly national and representative in character.

A significant number of women journalists are very successful in magazines dealing with various problems of women and child. With sensitivity and skill for analyzing events in depth, issues such as women abuse and exploitation, harassment of women at workplace and the trauma of HIV infected women, female infanticide in rural areas find a prominent place in such magazines. The magazines deal with the issues more in depth compared to newspapers and women are considered competent to handle such stories.

It is noticed that more and more young graduates are joining the journalism degree and diploma courses, with an ambition to make a mark in the profession, and quite a good proportion of them are girls. With the rapid expansion, almost a proliferation of the electronic media through satellite channels, with the popularity of the FM on the radio and with the growth of the print media, notwithstanding the electronic media, now there is a good scope for absorption of both men and women qualified journalists in various media outlets. Women, young and old, are prepared to weather the risks. The society, therefore, must make arrangements to provide adequate security to the vulnerable section of women in the media to promote their participation at all levels.

Recommendations and Suggestions

Certain recommendations were made by the Joshi Committee regarding positive portrayal of women on

Doordarshan[1]. But these recommendations are equally relevant to all form of media. These recommendations, if followed in letter and spirit would certainly go in long way in enhancement of women's empowerment and facilitate drastic reduction in cultural biases as well as gender biases[2]. They are

1. The women's issue one of the utmost significance to the country as a whole and there is need for a widespread understanding that the nation cannot progress, as long as women are left behind as the lesser half of society. Therefore, the improvement of women's conditions, status and image must be defined to be a major objective for media channels.

2. The Government must at the earliest formulate clear guidelines regarding the positive portrayal of women on television. This portrayal must take note of women in all facets of their lives: as workers and significant contributions to family survival and the national economy: it must further endeavour to integrate women on terms of equality in all sectors of national life and the development process. These guidelines must emphasise that the "women's dimension" must from an integral part of all programmes and not be merely confined to Women's Programmes, nor to isolated attempts to discuss women's issues.

3. The number of commercial formula films screened must be drastically reduced, the cheap song-and-dance sequence totally eliminated and the content of such programmes carefully scrutinized in terms of their portrayal of women.

4. Women must not be portrayed in stereotyped images that emphasis passive, submissive qualities and encourage them to play a subordinate secondary role in the family and society. Both men and women should be portrayed in ways that encourage mutual respect and a spirit of give and take between the sexes.

5. The foreign exchange resource should be spent on importing worthwhile educative programmes, particularly those that show the roles, lives and struggles of women in neighbouring and other Third World countries so that a greater understanding and a shared perspective on problems is built.

6. It is necessary to ensure that a large number of rural women gain access to TV. Therefore, in the placement of community TV sets preference should be given to the meeting place of Mandals; Mahila Mandals should also be involved in the community viewing arrangement." Everywhere the media has the potential to make a far greater contribution to the advancement of women. They can create self-regulatory mechanisms that can help to eliminate misleading and improper gender based programming.

Conclusion

Media is an agent to alarm policy makers to give immediate attention to gender related problems such as the adverse sex ratio, infant and maternal mortality, crime against women, gender violence, acid attack, dowry related problems, problems of the girl child, women labour problems, effects of poverty on women and their families. Unfortunately such coverage is very less in compared to the space covered by cinema, actresses, models, advertisements, glamour, beauty aids, cookery and fashion. The struggle for a fair and just portrayal of women in media is an ethical duty of the Fourth Estate. It is also accountable to the people and it is to act as a watchdog and guardian of the public interest. As an important agent of socialization shaping of gender roles, its mechanisms for checks and balances with respect to gender need to be strengthened. The media should enable projection of women in a decent and dignified way and promote respect and dignity to women avoiding negative portrayal of women. The media professionals need to be sensitised on gender issues and a system of rewards may be developed for those who are able to portray women in positive manner. Likewise, stringent punitive action should be taken against those who defy the norms. New innovative decent presentation of women, based on Indian culture and society through media must be introduced. A strong legislative effort coupled with a wide spread social awareness with morality and ethics is needed to fight this menace so that women are not perceived as a commodity but as individual with right and dignity.

Notes

1 Purnima Ojha, Women's Issues in India: Role and Importance of Media, The Indian Journal of Political Science, Vol. LXXII, No.I, Jan-March, 2011, pp.87-102

2 https://www.ohchr.org/EN/Issues/Women/Pages/InternationalStandards.aspx

3 Mamta Rao. Law relating to Women and child. (2012) 3rd. Ed. Eastern Book Co. .Lucknow. p. 224

4 Dr. Pranita Choudhury, Role of Media and Indecent Represesentation of Women, *IOSR Journal Of Humanities And Social Science (IOSR-JHSS) Volume 19, Issue 11, Ver. VIII (Nov. 2014), PP 33-36 e-ISSN: 2279-0837, p-ISSN: 2279-0845.*

5 http://www.legalserviceindia.com/article/l210-Law,-Women-And-Advertisements.html

6 Joshi Committee Report(1984).

7 Address by Mr. Justice G.N. Ray, Chairman, Press Council of India at the inauguration session of National Press Day on November 16, 2008 at Vigyan Bhawan, New Delhi.

6

Role of Sexual Disparity in Work Family Conflicts

Dr. Parul Sharda

Associate Professor, Indore Management Institute & Research Centre

Abstract: The way that the penetrability among family and work scopes produces work-family conflict (WFC) is entrenched. Accordingly, this chapter plans to check whether the inconsistent contribution in family tasks among people is related with expanded WFC in females and males, deciphering the outcomes additionally from the information that emerge from sex examines. A correlational study conducted with the help of questionnaire and collected 515 samples (63% males) of Indians without emotional relationship, who lived with their hetero accomplice. True to form, results right off the bat show inconsistent contribution in family errands by ladies and men as it is higher in ladies that in men, and the view of accomplice inclusion is lower in ladies that in men. Also, those inconsistent inclusions relate distinctively to people on various methods of work-family cooperation. They don't expand WFC in ladies contrasting with men, despite the fact that there are digressively critical contrasts in workplace conflict (WC) and factually huge in family conflict (FC). Be that as it may, impression of accomplice inclusion on family unit tasks expands WFC both in men and in ladies yet not WC nor FC. By and by, increment on marital conflict (MC) by homegrown assignments neither effect in a critical manner WFC in ladies nor in men, however increment WC in the two ladies and men and FC just in ladies. Results likewise affirm that subject contribution on family errands is certifiably not a critical indicator of WFC in ladies nor in men, and that MC by homegrown assignments is a factually huge indicator in ladies of

WFC and FC, yet not in men. In this manner, results show that conventional sexual orientation jobs actually influence the manner in which people deal with the work and family communication, in spite of the fact that the expanded WFC because of inclusion in housework isn't selective to ladies, yet in addition happens in men. Individual and institutional proposals are made based on these outcomes to adapt to these contentions.

Keywords: *sexual disparity, work-family conflict, marital conflict*

Introduction

Word related wellbeing brain research advances work hazard anticipation mediating both on the association and on the individual, yet additionally on work-family interface. It looks for the integrity of-fit among these measurements to lessen psychosocial hazards on word related wellbeing and simultaneously to improve hierarchical adequacy. The impact of psychosocial stressors at work doesn't stay inside the working circle as it stretches out likewise to individual life. This penetrability among family and work scopes has created work-family struggle (WFC) to be one of the psychosocial chances accepting more consideration during the previous years (Eby et al., 2005; Ammons and Kelly, 2015; French et al., 2017; Lapierre et al., 2017; Wayne et al., 2017; Carvalho et al., 2018). WFC adversely influences both wellbeing and general life, for example, work execution and work fulfilment inside the hierarchical setting, yet it additionally expands struggle rates and diminishes family fulfilment. From this point of view, and inside a setting of a more innovative and digitalized society, sexual orientation balance at work involves foremost significance, which must begin with a sex correspondence at home. The point of this investigation is to check whether the inconsistent inclusion in family unit errands among people is related with expanded WFC in ladies, and clarify it in wording incorporating the information on sexual orientation considers.

Work-Home Conflict and Gender

People may encounter strife between their work and home parts because of restricted time, elevated levels of pressure, and contending social desires (Greenhaus and Beutell, 1985). Albeit a large portion of the work-home exploration has zeroed in on how work factors influence home from the perspective of the contention between the two circles (Major and Cleveland, 2005), hierarchical brain science likewise starts to concentrate how family factors influence work execution and fulfillment.

In the psychosocial logical writing, there is a wide custom on the work and home interface examines (i.e., Kopelmanœ et al., 1983; Edwards and Rothbard, 2000; Pitt-Catsouphes et al., 2006; Mills, 2015; Paulin et al., 2017). Two essential points of view have been offered in this writing dependent on the contrariness between people's work and home spaces (Michel and Hargis, 2008). One viewpoint centers around the systems that produce strife between the two areas. The other point of view centers around the division components between the work and the family spaces. In this investigation, we receive the contention model in inspecting the impact of home jobs (differential inclusion of people on family tasks), on work jobs.

Some exploration has demonstrated that job pressure in work and home areas produces negative outcomes on the other one bidirectionally. So the level of support in the home job will make challenges for cooperation in work, bringing about the house-work conflict(HWC); then again, the level of investment in the work area can upset execution on the family job, delivering an expansion of strain-based, time sensitive or conduct based work-home conflict(WHC) (Huang et al., 2004).

Distinctive meta-investigations (Byron, 2005; Eby et al., 2005) have exhibited the key pretended by sex, yet how it identifies with work-family builds is as yet both hypothetically and exactly discussed (Shockley et al., 2017). Examination has discovered contrasts in work-home clash consistently, going from contrasts in the experience of WFC to the presence of various work and home foundations to ladies and men. In any case, most examinations in the field of work-home interface don't think about sex as a variable, recognizing all things considered corresponds and differential relationship for people (Martínez and Paterna, 2009). Along these lines, we place that work-home interface studies ought to incorporate sex as key variable because of the impact of sex philosophy and sex job direction may have on the work-home relationship from a social perspective.

From a social and desultory point of view (Gerstel and Sarkisian, 2006), sexual orientation philosophy, characterized as convictions and qualities kept up about what is ideal for people, decides the examples by which a specific culture judges or assesses the correct lead of a man or a lady.

This sex philosophy is additionally reflected in the social talk, as every now and again the couple reproduces the prevailing social talk wherein is alluded the fundamental qualities in which people vary disregarding the sociopolitical setting. This talk expresses that the contrasts among people according to home and work are the consequence of individual decision, that there are contrasts in natural capacities of people for family unit tasks and work outside the home, and that these distinctions control the decision for specific positions and even that inclination for home toward work is a free decision on account of ladies (Martínez and Paterna, 2009; Kuo et al., 2018). Connected to this philosophy, the customary sexual orientation good example endorses that work space and instrumentality are more significant for men than for ladies, while the home area and expressiveness is more significant for ladies. The customary sex good example has a biosocial and social root, and was portrayed by Parsons and Bales (1955) in their depiction of instrumental (men) and expressive (ladies) jobs. This model discretionarily accepts that expressiveness and instrumentality are independent measurements, and that expressiveness is consistently ladies sex job though instrumentality is that of men. Work and family collaborations are implanted in the more extensive social, institutional and monetary setting in which people live (Ollier-Malaterre and Foucreault, 2017). Of specific importance to sexual orientation contrasts in WFC are social contrasts in sex libertarianism, or conviction or perspectives about de balance of the genders inside de culture (House et al., 2004; Lucas-Thompson and Goldberg, 2015).

As Martínez and Paterna (2009) show, sexual orientation philosophy appears to decide the level of undertakings thought about generally ladylike by individuals from the couple, for example, washing, pressing, shopping, cooking, or cleaning. It additionally produces a differential importance about family errands for people. Likewise, late investigations have indicated that there is as yet a division of house errands by sex, contingent upon the sexual orientation job cores: instrumentality inside and outside home for men; expressiveness and instrumentality inside home for ladies (Fernández et al., 2016). This reasoning, drives us to figure hypotheses 1:

H1: There will be a division of family errands among people dependent on conventional sexual orientation jobs. Ladies will invest more energy than men in generally female family errands and men in customarily male ones.

The two people likewise see an absence of equality in performing family tasks, however see more noteworthy correspondence under the watchful eye of little girls and children (Yago and Martínez, 2009). This leads us to propose hypotheses 2:

H2: Women will see their accomplices significantly less associated with family unit errands and just spotlight on family unit tasks customarily viewed as manly. Men will see their female accomplices more engaged with customarily female family tasks, particularly in those generally viewed as ladylike.

Suggestion in Household Chores and Work-Family Conflict (WFC)

Time needed for family unit errands and thinking about the family is one of the main variables in the contention coming from the family circle, particularly in families with youngsters. Thus, the double pay couples with youngsters will in general have a more noteworthy number of contentions between the accomplices and a more elevated level of pressure than their partners without kids (Michel and Hargis, 2008). Starting here of view, the sexual orientation jobs model accepts that the idea of the job requests contrasts in people, and these jobs go about as mediators of WFC (Barnett et al., 1995).

The most significant level of family to work obstruction in ladies comes from the distinctive ramifications of ladies and men in family tasks, including the consideration of youngsters. This distinctive ramification has been demonstrated by different investigations and exploration (Bianchi et al., 2000; Korabik, 2015; Borelli et al., 2017) and still perseveres in the public eye as has been found in various studies (Organization for Economic Cooperation and Development [OECD], 2014; Eurobarometer, 2015). In solid, this model keeps persevering in India, where ladies spend practically twofold the measure of time on unpaid work as men National Institute of Statistics (INE), 2018). This time is spent on exercises, for example, thinking about kids (38 h seven days ladies versus 23 men) or relatives (20 h ladies versus 14 men) or family errands (20 h ladies versus 11 men). So, in spite of the fact that ladies have started to firmly frame a piece of the workforce and to invest more energy with their youngsters dealing with them, they neither accept a reduction in their compensation as much as ladies accomplish for work interferences because of family issues nor remain at home to deal with their kids (Gerstel and Sarkisian, 2006). Most men actually keep up full contribution in their work in light of the fact that their female couple accept the accountability for caring their youngsters. In this manner, we can find that ladies will endure more by the impedance of the family grinding away, on the grounds that their more noteworthy contribution in the family will can deduct them time, quality and commitment to their work; in any case, men will endure more by the obstruction of work in the family. Indeed, a high ramification in the family circle has been demonstrated connected to a higher family-to-work obstruction just in ladies (Hammer et al., 1997).

Additionally, men don't feel a commitment when they are engaged with the home as ladies do, as they see it more as a side interest or a free decision. Likewise, those house errands that keep the home each day (shopping, cooking, washing dishes, washing garments, and cleaning the house) are viewed as female, while those thought about male or impartial undertakings (taking care of tabs, dealing with the vehicle or home support) don't include day by day dedication. Some social understanding contend that ladies are more engaged with house errands and don't have any desire to completely share as a result of the conviction that this is fundamental to their sexual orientation character and a wellspring of intensity in the family, while spouses, whose sex personality has generally been set apart by paid work, would not protest do less family tasks than their wives (Martínez and Paterna, 2009).

Plus, a hybrid impact must be incorporated: to the more prominent contribution of ladies in the family and family errands must be added the best association of men in the work environment (Bakker et al., 2008), which guesses an expanded family trouble for ladies. As spouses are not accessible for family unit tasks, wives endure over-burden by family errands and enthusiastic requests identified with kids providing care, which will build even more ladies stress and family to work obstruction (Frone, 2003).

So, the lesser inclusion of men in family tasks and more prominent exchange of pressure from work to family causes expanded homegrown remaining burden on ladies and Marital Conflicts (MC), in this way expanding the strain move from family climate to worksite in ladies. This reasoning, drives us to plan hypotheses 3:

H3: The more prominent association of ladies in family errands and the impression of the lesser inclusion of their men accomplices is connected to an expanded family to work strife (FWC) in ladies.

Marital Conflicts and Household Chores

This more noteworthy contribution of ladies in family ensemble and expanded family to work struggle may prompt an expansion of MC. In this line, Pittman et al. (1996) give proof to this thought by indicating that the commitment of ladies to family unit tasks is higher when their spouses express more

couple with offspring of young, excluding others that might be less successive in this culture (i.e., cutting the grass).

- Partner association in family errands discernment scale. This self-built scale is like the one above, yet for this situation it gauges the subjects' impression of their accomplices' association in all the family tasks. Subjects react to everything utilizing a dichotomous yes/no organization about their view of their accomplice's association in various family undertakings. The last scale score is the absolute number of errands they see that their accomplices devote to family assignments. An illustration of these things is Does your accomplice take the youngsters to class in regular daily existence?
- Marital clash about family errands was estimated with the single inquiry what number occasions do you and your accomplice contend about who must do the family unit tasks and when? Subjects react to this thing on a Likert scale going from 1 (never) to 5 (consistently).

We additionally estimated socio-segment (sex and age) and socio-natural (family status, number of youngsters) factors for the example portrayal.

Data Analyses

To begin with, we performed skewness and kurtosis examinations to check ordinariness among factors. Second, we determined interior textures (Cronbach's á), clear investigations and connections between contention scales and subject/accomplice saw contribution on family tasks scales. Third, we figured Analyses of Variance (ANOVAs) to test whether there was any measurably critical contrast between-bunch with respect to sexual orientation for subject's contribution in family errands scale, and subject's view of accomplice's inclusion in family unit scale, and Kruskal–Wallis non-parametrical tests for thing to thing investigation because of its dichotomous degree of reaction (Hypothesis 1 and 2). From that point forward, we processed new ANOVAs and Regression Analyses to check sexual orientation, family unit errands, accomplice's suggestion and strife on WFC, WC, and FC (Hypothesis 3 and 4). All information examinations were completed utilizing SPSS 21.0.

Results

Table 1 shows skewness and kurtosis insights. True to form, all scales show esteems equivalent or underneath 0.5 and "0.5 in both or if nothing else at one of them. So, we expect a typical conveyance of the scores of these scales. In any case, thing by thing of subject's and accomplice's inclusion in family tasks scales don't follow that ordinary conveyance, because of its dichotomic nature.

Table 1: "Skewness and Kurtosis analysis of variables distribution."

	"Skewness"		"Kurtosis"	
	Statistics	*SE*	Statistics	*SE*
"Work-family conflict"	"0.02	0.11	"0.27	0.22
"Work conflict"	"0.20	0.11	"0.50	0.22
"Family conflict"	0.56	0.11	"0.16	0.22
"Marital conflict"	0.46	0.11	"0.80	0.22
"Involvement on household chores (total mean scale score)"				
"Subject involvement on household chores"	0.79	0.15	0.01	0.3
"Perception of partner involvement on household chores"	0.76	0.15	0.31	0.3
"Subject involvement on household chores (item to item)"				
"Home shopping"	0.92	0.11	"1.16	0.21
"Cleaning home"	0.38	0.11	"1.87	0.21
"Domestic repairing"	0.84	0.11	"1.30	0.21
"Family management"	0.69	0.11	"1.53	0.21
"Free time family management"	1.62	0.11	0.63	0.21
"Take children from home to school"	1.14	0.11	"0.71	0.21
"Take children from school to home"	1.19	0.11	"0.60	0.21
"Children caregiving"	0.73	0.11	"1.47	0.21
"Helping children with homework"	1.2	0.11	"0.57	0.21
"Playing with children"	3.6	0.11	10.85	0.21
"Perception of partner engagement and involvement on household chores (item to item)"				
"Home shopping"	2.1	0.11	2.37	0.21
"Cleaning home"	1.4	0.11	0.02	0.21
"Domestic repairing"	0.33	0.11	"1.90	0.21
"Family management"	1.22	0.11	"0.51	0.21
"Free time family management"	2.66	0.11	5.11	0.21
"Take children from home to school"	1.57	0.11	0.47	0.21
"Take children from school to home"	1.49	0.11	0.24	0.21
"Children caregiving"	1.97	0.11	1.92	0.21
"Helping children with homework"	2.13	0.11	2.58	0.21
"Playing with children"	4.43	0.11	17.7	0.21

Table 2-shows the graphic examinations and Cronbach's alpha of the factors for the two examples. The alpha qualities meet the basis of 0.70 (Nunnally and Bernstein, 1994), with the exception of the impression of accomplice's association in family unit errands, which was above 0.60. True to form, the example of connections shows that WFC, work strife and FC are decidedly and altogether related in the two examples. Be that as it may, WFC is more identified with strife at work in ladies and to struggle in the family in men.

Marital Conflicts is just exceptionally and emphatically identified with WFC, work strife and FC in ladies, yet not in men. This could demonstrate that ladies acclimatize the contention with the accomplice into clashes in the family, i.e., ladies incorporate the couple into the family idea, while men believe them to appear as something else.

Subject's inclusion in family errands connects huge and contrarily with WFC in the two people, yet just with work struggle in men. At that point, for the two people, the higher their association is in family tasks, the lower their WFC; also, the higher the work struggle is, the lower the men's contribution in family errands.

At long last, the relationship between the subject's and the impression of the accomplice's inclusion in family unit tasks is just profoundly, fundamentally and adversely related in ladies. Be that as it may, the view of the accomplice's association in family unit tasks is just profoundly, essentially and emphatically identified with WFC in men. Hence, ladies decline their contribution in family tasks when their male accomplices increment their inclusion; then again, on account of men, the more prominent the association of the accomplice (ladies) in the family unit errands, the higher the WFC is.

ANOVA results affirm these distinctions and imbalance about people's inclusion in family unit errands. Ladies' association in family unit tasks is more than twice that of men (4.0 and 1.7, separately; F = 82.60; p d" 001). Reliably, ladies see lower contribution of their accomplice (men) in family unit tasks than men do (1.8 and 2.8, individually; F = 22.70; p d" 001).

Kruskal–Wallis tests additionally affirm that ladies are altogether more required than men in seven of eleven family

Table 2: "Cronbach's alpha, means (*M*), standard deviation (*SD*), and intercorrelations by gender ($N = 515$)."

	"Women"								"Men"					
	α	*M*	*SD*	1	2	3	4	5	*M*	*SD*	1	2	3	4
(1) "Work-family conflict"	0.78	2.1	0.7						2	0.7				
(2) "Work conflict"	0.78	2.7	0.75	0.34"d					2.9	0.87	0.28"d			
(3) "Family conflict"	0.76	2.4	0.81	0.26""	0.30""				2.3	0.87	0.33""	0.40""		
(4) "Marital conflict"	–	2.4	1.3	0.31"d	0.21"d	0.42"d			2.2	1	"0.05	0.1	0.03	
(5) "Subject involvement on household chores"	0.72	4	0.15	"0.17"	"0.16	0.09	0.12		1.7	0.12	"0.18"d	"0.23"d	0.18	0.08
(6) "Perception of partner involvement on household chores"	0.62	1.8	0.98	0.14	0.14	0.04	"0.18	"0.49""	2.8	1.5	0.31""	0.02	0.08	"0.10

""$p < 0.01$, "$p < 0.05$.

unit tasks **(see Table 3).** These seven assignments are customarily viewed as female: home shopping, housekeeping, leisure time family the board, taking youngsters from home to class and from school to home, kids' consideration, helping kids with schoolwork, and playing with them. Men just score higher than ladies on one errand generally viewed as manly: house fixes. There are no distinctions in family the executives. These outcomes affirm Hypothesis 1.

Table 3: "Kruskal–Wallis test of subject involvement on household chores and perception of partner engagement on household chores by gender (item to item) (*N* = 515)."

	Women		Men			
	M	*SD*	*M*	*SD*	Chi-square	GL
"Subject engagement and involvement on household chores (item to item)"						
Home shopping	**0.4**	0.49	0.13	0.33	39.078""d	1
Cleaning home	**0.61**	0.49	0.05	0.22	153.846""d	1
Domestic repairing	0.1	0.3	**0.67**	0.47	180.924""d	1
Family management	0.31	0.47	0.38	0.49	2.455	1
Free time family management	**0.22**	0.41	0.13	0.33	6.725"d	1
Take children from home to school	**0.32**	0.47	0.13	0.34	22.959""d	1
Take children from school to home	**0.34**	0.47	0.08	0.28	41.483""d	1
Children caregiving	**0.5**	0.5	0.04	0.2	109.332""d	1
Helping children with homework	**0.35**	0.48	0.07	0.25	49.258""d	1
Playing with children	**0.1**	0.28	0.03	0.16	6.923""	1
"Perception of partner engagement and involvement on household chores (item to item)"						
Home shopping	0.08	0.28	**0.24**	0.43	24.355""d	1
Cleaning home	0.05	0.22	**0.5**	0.5	141.873""d	1
Domestic repairing	**0.64**	0.48	0.03	0.16	187.264""d	1
Family management	**0.3**	0.46	0.14	0.35	15.260""d	1
Free time family management	0.07	0.26	**0.15**	0.36	7.49""	1
Take children from home to school	0.12	0.33	**0.3**	0.46	24.446""d	1
Take children from school to home	0.1	0.31	**0.37**	0.48	51.522""d	1
Child caregiving	0.05	0.22	**0.32**	0.47	66.873""d	1
Helping children with homework	0.08	0.28	**0.23**	0.42	21.669""d	1
Playing with children	0.04	0.2	0.04	0.2	0	1

The highest values, when significant, appear in bold. ""dp dd 001, ""p dd 01.

Evenly, Kruskal–Wallis tests likewise show that these outcomes are affirmed by the observation that people have of their accomplice's contribution in family unit tasks: men think about that their accomplices (ladies) are fundamentally associated with customarily ladylike family errands: home shopping, housekeeping, extra time family the executives, taking kids from home to class and school to home, dealing with the youngsters, and helping kids with schoolwork, while ladies think about that their accomplices (men) are engaged with regularly manly family tasks: house fixes and family the board. There are no distinctions in the view of playing with the kids. All in all, these outcomes affirm Hypothesis 2.

To test the speculation 3 (the impact of the more prominent contribution of ladies in family errands and view of lesser association of male accomplices in the expansion in the WFC among ladies contrasted with men), and theory 4 (the impact of MC in the expanded degree of WFC in ladies comparative with men), we performed three separate ANOVAs **(Table 4),** supplemented by different relapse examination **(Table 5).**

Table 4: "Analysis of variance of work-family conflict, work conflict and family conflict by subject involvement on household chores and subject perception of partner involvement on household chores and marital conflict by gender (N = 515)."

Sex		"Work conflict"		"Family conflict"		"Work-family conflict"	
		M	*SD*	*M*	*SD*	*M*	*SD*
"Subject involvement on household chores"							
High	Women	2.7	0.98	2.8	1	2.2	0.85
	Men	3.9	0.27	3.1	0.85	2	0.87
Low	Women	2.9	0.69	2.6	0.8	2.4	0.72
	Men	3.2	0.9	2.1	0.92	2.3	0.71
	F	2.516+	3.552"	1.204			
"Perception of partner involvement on household chores"							
High	Women	2.9	0.35	2.9	1.1	2.7	0.53
	Men	3.8	0.53	2.6	0.92	2.4	0.66
Low	Women	2.6	0.84	2.5	0.9	2	0.77
	Men	3.3	0.93	2.6	0.95	1.8	0.68
	F	2.33	0.69	8.458""Š			
"Marital conflict"							
High	Women	2.9	0.77	3	0.8	2.3	0.74
	Men	3.8	0.85	2.6	0.71	2.1	0.54
Low	Women	2.7	0.76	2.4	0.7	2.3	0.67
	Men	3.4	0.89	2.6	1	2.2	0.78
	F	3.273""	7.442""	0.533			

""Šp d" 0.001, "dp d" 0.01, "p d" 0.05, +p d" 0.10.

Table 5: "Regression analyses predicting work conflict, family conflict and work-family conflict (dependent variables) in women and men by involvement on household chores, subject perception of partner involvement on household chores and level of marital conflict (independent variables)."

	"Work Conflict"		"Family Conflict"		"Work-Family Conflict"	
	Women	Men	Women	Men	Women	Men
	β	β	β	β	β	β
"Subject involvement on household chores"	0.09	0.15	"0.09	"0.20""	"0.10	"0.11
"Perception of partner involvement on house hold chores"	0.12"	0.09	0.08	0.01	0.08	0.23"
"Marital conflict"	0.42"d	0.02	0.22"d	0.11	0.26"	"0.03
	$R^2 = 0.18$""	$R^2 = 01$	$R^2 = 0.06$""	$R^2 = 0.02$	$R^2 = 0.07$""	$R^2 = 0.06$"

"dp < 0.01, "p < 0.05. Standardized beta coefficients (N = 515).

ANOVAs results affirm mostly speculation 3 since more noteworthy association of ladies in family unit errands don't produce a measurably huge expansion in WFC contrasting with men. There are sex contrasts in the degree to which this differential inclusion in homegrown undertakings influences FC and (in an extraneously huge way) WC that highlight a sex impact. On one hand, on account of ladies, when their association in family unit tasks is high, their FC and WC levels are comparable; nonetheless, when their inclusion is low, FC diminishes and WC increments. Then again, on account of men, the WC is consistently more noteworthy than the FC paying little mind to their level of inclusion in family unit tasks. That is, on account of ladies when there is a lower association in family unit errands the FC is additionally lower, yet builds the WC.

There are no sex contrasts with respect to the WFC as indicated by the impression of their accomplices: it increments altogether in the two people when the contribution in family errands of the accomplice is high or low, being consistently higher among ladies than among men paying little mind to the association of the cooperate with family unit tasks is high or low, which totally dismisses theory 3.

It is important that the impact of the impression of contribution of the accomplice in family unit errands by sexual orientation doesn't influence WC or FC in a sex explicit way, yet it influences the WFC internationally measurably fundamentally, in spite of the fact that these distinctions were not sex impacts show. This demonstrates that the WFC is influenced by the inclusion of the accomplice in family tasks, however not for the association of the subject in them, which segmentally would influence the FC and WC.

Concerning 4, the expansion of contention by homegrown errands among the accomplices doesn't influence the WFC in a factually critical manner in ladies nor in men, however it does on WC and FC: when MC is high WC increment both in ladies and men, yet FC increment just in ladies.

As an affirmation of this outcomes, with respect to the connection between the subject's and accomplice's contribution in family unit errands and the various clashes, relapse examinations (see Table Table55) show, first, that subject association on family unit tasks doesn't anticipate WFC in ladies nor men, yet just WC in men in a negative way. Also, the view of the accomplice's contribution in family errands and MC is an indicator of ladies' WC and men's WFC. Again, these outcomes don't affirm speculation 3.

All things considered, with respect to speculation 4, as a distinction of the ANOVA results, the expansion of contention by homegrown errands among the accomplices anticipate the WFC, WC, and FC in a measurably critical path in ladies however not in men. So results show that MC in ladies predicts WFC. This outcome completely uphold theory 4. Furthermore, the MC is the main variable of those examined that influences the FC on account of ladies, while inclusion in housework does on account of men, supporting likewise theory 4.

On account of men, the impression of the accomplice's (ladies) inclusion in family errands is an indicator of WFC. Results additionally show that men's inclusion in family unit tasks is a negative factually huge indicator FC as their beta coefficient is negative. That is, it appears to be that when the association of men in housework expands, the contention in the family diminishes; yet when the impression of contribution of their female accomplices is high, it increments in them the WFC. Be that as it may, MC doesn't foresee this FC in men, so the FC doesn't increment by the contention with the accomplice for housework yet by their low contribution in them.

Discussions

Home-work collaboration has been the focal point of a wide scope of logical writing during the previous many years. It is commonly acknowledged that both the family and the work scope influence each other in an alternate manner. Notwithstanding, it was not concentrated in which degree the own and the accomplice's association in family gives influence distinctive sort of work-home clash from a sex perspective. Along these lines, the point of this examination was to check whether the inconsistent inclusion in family errands among people is related with expanded WFC in ladies, and clarify it in wording incorporating the information on sexual orientation considers.

All things considered, more than twofold the association of their male accomplices. Moreover, men are more associated with generally manly family tasks (i.e., home fixes and family the executives), and ladies are more associated with customarily ladylike errands (i.e., childcare or shopping). Evenly, the subject's impression of the accomplice suggestion affirms this distinction: ladies view of their men accomplice association in family errands substantially less than men view of their lady accomplice inclusion. Thusly, theories 1 and 2 of our examination are affirmed.

Furthermore, we checked if those inconsistent inclusions relate distinctively to people on various methods of WF connection. We found that the more prominent inclusion of ladies in family unit tasks doesn't influence the degree of WFC differentially in people, so speculation 3 isn't met. This sexual orientation imbalance in the dispersion of family errands and youngster care doesn't infer a more significant level of WFC in ladies contrasted with men. Or maybe the inverse occurs: when more included are the two people in family errands, lower is the WFC. In spite of the fact that the theory 3 isn't certified, it should be noticed that when the inclusion of ladies in family errands is high, their degree of FC increments; when men's association builds, their degree of WC expands, which here and there underpins speculation 3. That is, the high inclusion in family unit errands has negative outcomes in the family circle for ladies and in the work environment for men, potentially in light of the more noteworthy particular significance that ladies provide for family and men to work, as it represents the conventional sex good example.

Moreover, results show that when the contribution of ladies in family unit tasks is high, their degrees of WC and FC are comparative, i.e., it similarly influences the two territories. At the point when this association is low, FC is lower than the WC. Notwithstanding, among men, WC is consistently more prominent than the WC paying little heed to their contribution in family tasks. Moreover, when the contention with the accomplice for family unit tasks is high, ladies report a higher FC however not a higher WC, though in man this contention doesn't influence neither the FC nor the WC.

Be that as it may, on account of ladies, MC influences struggle related WC and FC and WFC, so theory 4 is completely authenticated. This is exceptionally intriguing in light of the fact that despite the fact that theory 3 isn't met, in any case, the contention with the accomplice because of this disparity in the appropriation of housework appears to produce this WFC. That is, it would not be simply the best association in family tasks that may cause and build WFC in ladies, however the contention with their accomplice which may deliver it.

These outcomes might be identified with the nonattendance of view of bad form in the connections in regards to disparity in the appropriation of homegrown and family obligations among people, so that by and large ladies neither do see shamefulness in their connections nor are disappointed. Following the audit of Yago and Martínez (2009), it has more than once indicated that the impression of an inconsistent conveyance of housework among people doesn't really prompt a view of shamefulness. This view of equity on the division of homegrown work and the philosophy of conventional sex that upholds it clarify why sexual orientation imbalances stay in the family circle intervening the connection between the impression of foul play and saw quality the relationship. Truth be told, when ladies are all the more socially and genuinely free from their accomplices, they are bound to think about unjustifiable the disparity in the dissemination of family unit errands.

The impression of treachery is an interceding factor between an inconsistent circulation of homegrown work and the apparent nature of the relationship; the relationship might be seen as acceptable despite the fact that the sharing of obligations isn't equivalent, on the off chance that it isn't seen uncalled for (Yago and Martínez, 2009). Notwithstanding, these outcomes were interceded by sexual orientation belief system so this inequal conveyance don't produce trouble in the more customary ladies though it does in ladies with an equivalent sex philosophy.

In this line an investigation of Ogolsky et al. (2014) shows that the errors at an intellectual level among people as to uniformity in family unit tasks influences the nature of the relationship in the circle of the couple in more noteworthy manner to ladies than in men. Be that as it may, when this imbalance is showed in a social level, it doesn't appear to influence the nature of the relationship in ladies. That is, the genuine imbalance doesn't influence the nature of the relationship in ladies, however it does at the intellectual level.

The association of the couple in family tasks is identified with an expanded WFC, despite the fact that it doesn't influence the WC or the FC independently by sexual orientation, however influences the WFC around the world: it increments comparably in people when the couple's contribution is high. This demonstrates that the WFC is influenced by the association of the accomplice in family errands, however not for the contribution of the subject in them, which would influence to a portioned FC and WC. These outcomes don't demonstrate the speculation 3, yet can show that the model of customary sexual orientation jobs doesn't serve to sufficiently clarify the impact of the division of family errands and the impact of sex imbalance in the WFC, as both on account of people more engaged with family unit tasks produce that their female and male accomplices feel an expanded WFC.

People's impression of their accomplices' inclusion in family errands contribute essentially to the view of WFC; their own association likewise contributes fundamentally to FC, yet contrarily, which implies that the more elaborate their accomplice is in the family unit tasks, the more prominent their WFC.

In spite of the fact that our examination appears to show that sex is a significant variable in the association in family errands, and that sex disparity and the model of customary sexual orientation jobs is as yet legitimate in our western culture, it likewise implies that expanded WFC because of a high contribution in family tasks isn't selective to men yet additionally happens in ladies. This could be a pointer of an adjustment in the model of customary sexual orientation jobs that started during the 80s, where new ages compare the significance of work and family circles in the instances of the two people.

Indeed, aftereffects of some ongoing exploration (Shockley et al., 2017) demonstrate that people seem, by all accounts, to be more comparable than various in their WFC encounters; sex contrasts in WFC appear to commonly be little, paying little mind to which explicit subgroups are inspected, and when there is significant variety in the greatness of sex contrasts in WFC the key factors that decide this variety is right now not surely knew.

Starting here of view, a few elective models other than the contention viewpoint may clarify these outcomes. This tis the instance of models, for example, the cooperative energy among work and family, positive equilibrium, work-family help, or work-family advancement (Beutell and Wittig-Berman, 2008; Lapierre et al., 2017), which would better comprehend the impact of sex on the person's connection among work and family.

The utilization of this new model integrative methodology is advocated by the social changes that portray the estimations of the new ages, Gen Xers (conceived somewhere in the range of 80 and 2000 populace). They appear to consider that both work and family are similarly significant in their life, and attempt to locate the most suitable approach to accommodate the two angles (Beutell and Wittig-Berman, 2008), giving less significance to presentism at work and being allies of adaptability. This comprehension of the work is based, notwithstanding the offices gave the computerized transformation and advances for work, making laborers less needy of a specific actual space and a fixed timetable to play out their work, along with the estimations of individual self-sufficiency and obligation that are shared by this new age. This encourages that individuals would now be able to have more opportunity to dedicate to different aspects of their life inside the extent of non-work, for example, family or relaxation, with a continuously more prominent significance in their social character.

Starting here of view, research on work and family collaboration has developed from the investigation of secluded factors inside the contention and division models toward more intricate models that attempt to comprehend from the limit hypothesis, and the models of assistance and cooperative energy, how advances are produced using one degree to the next, and how they coordinate with one another. They don't think about them as independent areas yet as something unitary and tough inside the life of individuals. Similarly, a methodology that considers the sexual orientation philosophy is dynamically being forced, since it is indistinguishable from the connection among work and the family from a social perspective.

Limitations of the Study

This examination centres around the impact of various types of contention identified with the home and work settings. Notwithstanding, due the absence of clear contrasts in outcomes with respect to WFC in people when accomplices' suggestion in family chorale is high, it is important to incorporate assistance and cooperative energy models that would make it more obvious the work-family relationship in the entirety of its features, including the pretended by sexual orientation and sex disparity. Examination on the positive complementary impacts of work and family is essential to understanding the multifaceted nature of the work-family collaboration.

Also, this investigation has other methodological constraints. To begin with, we contemplated the impact of sexual orientation and inclusion in family unit tasks on the work-family relationship utilizing free examples of people, without gathering information from their accomplices. Nonetheless, we broke down the impression of these individuals (people) about their own association and their accomplice's contribution, and this discernment was demonstrated to be critical. All things considered, it is fascinating to remember the entire couple as a unit for future examinations to build the dependability of the proposed model.

Second, this investigation depends just on quantitative examinations. It is intriguing to help these outcomes with subjective examinations (through meetings or centre gatherings) that would assist us with interpreting the investigations of the outcomes outlined in both the customary sex jobs and cross-impact speculations, yet in addition in individuals' translations, expanding the model's legitimacy. They would likewise permit us to comprehend the sexual orientation function toward the cross-impacts of work pressure from men to ladies, or from ladies to men, as our outcomes just mostly uphold this cross-impact, in spite of past outcomes (Bakker et al., 2008). Regardless, the quantitative strategy utilized in this investigation permitted us to recognize, in a moderately straightforward way, the presence of changes in the connection among sexual orientation and the conventional division of functions as an initial step.

Additionally, the family unit errands utilized are those that may be summed up to generally couples with youngsters at young. In any case, we have not thought about explicit circumstances (i.e., living in their home, living in an enormous or in an unassuming community, grandparents uphold in caring kids, age of the youngsters) that may have help us to all the more likely depict the example and decipher our outcomes. Future examinations could incorporate this sort of sociodemographic factors.

Also, might be other methodological impediments that may have adapted the outcomes. One of them is the unevenness in the level of men (63%) with respect to ladies (37%). Be that as it may, this impediment is probable given the correlational idea of the examination and the expansiveness of the example. At last, the dependably of the contribution of the accomplice in family unit errands isn't excessively high (Cronbach's alpha 0.62) which could raise questions about its impact as an autonomous variable in the WFC in men and WC among ladies. All things considered, it met generally acknowledged rules to accept its dependably (over 0.60).

Pragmatic Implications

These outcomes raise various down to earth suggestions for equity among people regarding sexual orientation issues in the powerful administration of associations to set up social reconciliation and fairness arrangements in both family and work settings (Wharton, 2015). The administration of work and working time inside associations must consider the social changes happening in sex jobs, and begin to consider that the two people progressively will in general give similar significance to their work and family conditions (Kuo et al., 2018) with the going with increment in WFC and stress in the two accomplices.

Subsequently, albeit much of the time conventional sexual orientation jobs are as yet substantial (the family circle keeps on being more significant for ladies than for men), it is important to consider the vision and explicit mentalities that the two specialists have about their inclusion in work and family, and set up authoritative strategies that help to accommodate the two circles in the two sexes (Lucas-Thompson and Goldberg, 2015).

Besides, public and social foundations spend significant time in family matters should join these reformist changes in conventional sex parts into their techniques, to encourage the homogenization of ladies' and men's functions inside the family and work environment. For example, they can configuration family guiding and couple preparing efforts that help them to find how to best facilitate their devotion to the family such that will diminish pressure and struggle, and how to limit WFC, in any event, making an interpretation of it into work-family cooperative energy.

Yet additionally associations may take an interest in this social change. They may contribute for example through the incorporation of family cordial legislative issues to help the quest for home-work equilibrium of their laborers, people (Sprung et al., 2015; Lin et al., 2017; Matias et al., 2017). It would mean an approach to improve the nature of working existence of their laborers and, simultaneously, an arrival of venture (ROI) both for the association (Dowd et al., 2017) and for our, ideally, every time fairer society.

References:

1. Ammons S. K., Kelly E. L. eds (2015). Work and Family in the New Economy. Exploration in the Sociology of Work Vol. 26 Bingley: Emerald Group Publishing Limited; 10.1108/S0277-283320150000026006 [CrossRef] [Google Scholar]

2. Bakker A. B., Dollard M. F., Demeroutti E. (2008). How employment requests influence accomplices' experience of depletion: incorporating work-family struggle and hybrid hypothesis. J. Appl. Psychol. 93 901–911. 10.1037/0021-9010.93.4.901 [PubMed] [CrossRef] [Google Scholar]

3. Barnett R. C., Raudenbush S. W., Brennan R. T., Pleck J. H., Marshall N. L. (1995). Changes in work and conjugal experience and change in mental misery: a longitudinal investigation of double worker couples. J. Pers. Soc. Psychol. 69 839–850. 10.1037/0022-3514.69.5.839 [PubMed] [CrossRef] [Google Scholar]

4. Beutell N. J., Wittig-Berman U. (2008). Work-family strife and work-family cooperative energy for age X, gen X-ers, and develops. J. Administrative Psychol. 23 507–523. 10.1108/02683940810884513 [CrossRef] [Google Scholar]

5. Bianchi S. M., Milkie M. A., Sayer L. C., Robinson J. P. (2000). Is it true that anyone is doing the housework? Patterns in the sex division of family work. Soc. Powers 79 191–228. 10.1093/sf/79.1.191 [CrossRef] [Google Scholar]

6. Borelli J. L., Nelson S. K., River L. M., Birken S. A., Moss-Racusin C. (2017). Sexual orientation contrasts in work-family coerce in guardians of small kids. Sex Roles 76 356–368. 10.1007/s11199-016-0579-0 [CrossRef] [Google Scholar]

7. Byron K. (2005). A meta-diagnostic survey of work-family strife and its forerunners. J. Vocat. Behav. 67 169–198. 10.1016/j.jvb.2004.08.009 [CrossRef] [Google Scholar]

8. Carvalho V. S., Chambel M. J., Neto M., Lopes S. (2018). Accomplishes work-family con?ict intercede the relationship of occupation qualities with representatives' emotional well-being among people? Front. Psychol. 9:966. 10.3389/fpsyg.2018.00966 [PMC free article] [PubMed] [CrossRef] [Google Scholar]

9. Dowd W. N., Bray J. W., Barbosa C., Brockwood K., Kaiser D. J., Mills M. J., et al. (2017). Cost and rate of profitability of a work-family intercession in the all-inclusive consideration industry: proof from the work, family and wellbeing netwrok. J. Occup. Environ. Medications. 59 956–965. 10.1097/JOM.0000000000001097 [PMC free article] [PubMed] [CrossRef] [Google Scholar]

10. Eby L. T., Casper W. J., Lockwood A., Bordeaux C., Brinley A. (2005). Work and family research in IO/OB: content examination and audit of the writing (1980–2002). J. Vocat. Behav. 66 124–197. 10.1016/j.jvb.2003.11.003 [CrossRef] [Google Scholar]

11. Edwards J. R, Rothbard N. P. (2000). Components connecting work and family: explaining the connection among work and family develops. Acad. Oversee. Fire up. 25 178–199. 10.5465/amr.2000.2791609 [CrossRef] [Google Scholar]

12. Eurobarometer (2015). Sexual orientation fairness report. Unique Eurobarometer 428/Wave EB82.4 – TNS Opinion and Social, March 2015. Accessible at: http://ec.europa.eu/equity/sexual orientation fairness/records/archives/eurobarometer_report_2015_en.pdf [Google Scholar]

13. Fernández J., Quiroga M. A., Escorial S., Privado J. (2016). The gendered division of family tasks. Psicothema 28 130–136. [PubMed] [Google Scholar]

14. French K. A., Dumani S., Allen T. D., Shockley K. M. (2017). A meta-investigation of work-family struggle and social help. Psychol. Bull. 144 284–314. 10.1037/bul0000120 [PMC free article] [PubMed] [CrossRef] [Google Scholar]

15. Frone M. R. (2003). "Work-family balance," in Handbook of Occupational Health Psychology, eds Quick J. C., Tetrick L. E. (Washington, DC: American Psychological Association;), 143–162. 10.1037/10474-007 [CrossRef] [Google Scholar]

16. Greenhaus J. H., Beutell N. J. (1985). Wellsprings of contention among work and family jobs. Acad. Oversee. Fire up. 10 76–88. 10.2307/258214 [CrossRef] [Google Scholar]

17. Gerstel N., Sarkisian N. (2006). "Sociological points of view on families and work: the import of sex, class and race," in The Work and Family Handbook: Multi-Disciplinary Perspectives and Approaches, eds Pitt-Catsouphes M., Kossek E. E., Sweet S. (Mahwah, NJ: LEA;), 237–267. [Google Scholar]

18. Mallet L. B., Allen B., Grigsby T. D. (1997). Work-family struggle in double worker couples: Within-individual and hybrid impacts of work and family. J. Vocat. Behav. 50 185–203. 10.1006/jvbe.1996.1557 [CrossRef] [Google Scholar]

19. House R. J., Hanges P. J., Javidan M., Dorfman P. W., Gupta V. (2004). Culture, Leadership, and Organizations: The GLOBE Study of 62 Societies. New York: Sage Publications. [Google Scholar]

20. Huang Y. H., Hammer L. B., Neal M. B., Parrin N. A. (2004). The connection between work-to-family struggle and family-to-work strife: a longitudinal. Study J. Fam. Econ. Issues 25 79–100. 10.1023/ B:JEEI.0000016724.76936.a1 [CrossRef] [Google Scholar]

21. Huffman A. H., Matthews R. A., Irving L. H. (2017). Family reasonableness and attachment in conjugal dyads: interceding measures between work-family strife and couple mental trouble. J. Occupat. Organ. Psychol. 90 95–116. 10.1111/joop.12165 [CrossRef] [Google Scholar]

22. Kahn R. L., Wolfe D. M., Quinn R. P., Snoek J. D., Rosenthal R. A. (1964). Authoritative Stress Studies in Role Conflict and Ambiguity. New York, NY: Wiley. [Google Scholar]

23. Kopelmanœ R. E., Greenhaus J. H., Connolly T. F. (1983). A model of work, family, and interrole strife: a build approval study. Organ. Beav. Murmur. Perform. 32 198–215. 10.1016/0030-5073(83)90147-2 [CrossRef] [Google Scholar]

24. Korabik K. (2015). "The crossing point of sex and work-family coerce," in Gender and the Work-Family Experience, ed. Factories M. (Cham: Springer;). [Google Scholar]

25. Kuo P. X., Volling B. L., González R. (2018). Sexual orientation Role Beliefs, work-family strife, and father association after the introduction of a subsequent youngster. Psychol. Men Masculinity 19 243–256. 10.1037/men0000101 [PMC free article] [PubMed] [CrossRef] [Google Scholar]

26. Lapierre L. M., Li Y., Kwang H. K., Greenhaus J. H., Di Renzo M. S., Shao P. (2017). A meta-investigation of the predecessors of work-family advancement. J. Organ. Behav. 39 385–401. 10.1002/job.2234 [CrossRef] [Google Scholar]

27. Lin K. J., Llies R., Pluut H., Pan S. Y. (2017). You are a useful collaborator, however do you uphold your mate? An asset based work-family model of aiding and backing arrangement. Organ. Behav. Murmur. Decis. Cycle. 138 45–58. 10.1016/ j.obhdp.2016.12.004 [CrossRef] [Google Scholar]

28. Lucas-Thompson R. G., Goldberg W. A. (2015). "Sex belief system and work-family plans of the future," in Gender and the Work-

Family Experience, ed. Factories M. (Cham: Springer;), 3–19. [Google Scholar]

29. Significant D. A., Cleveland J. N. (2005). "Mental viewpoints on the work-family interface," in Work, Family, Health, and Well-being, eds Bianchi M., Casper L. M., King B. R. (Mahwah, NJ: Lawrence Erlbaum Associates Publishers;), 169–186. [Google Scholar]

30. Martínez M. C., Paterna C. (2009). "Perspectiva de género aplicada a la conciliación (Gender point of view applied to work-family pacification)," in Género y Conciliación de la Vida Familiar y Laboral: Un análisis psicosocial, ed. Martínez M. C. (Murcia: Editum-Ediciones de la Universidad de Murcia;), 17–44. [Google Scholar]

31. Martínez-Pérez M. D., Osca A. (2001). Psychometric investigation of the Indian rendition of the work-family strife scale by kopelman, greenhaus and connoly, 1983. Fire up. Psicol. Soc. 16 43–58. 10.1174/021347401317351198 [CrossRef] [Google Scholar]

32. Matias M., Ferreira T., Vieira J., Cadima J., Leal T., Mena Matos P. (2017). Work environment family uphold, parental fulfillment, and work-family struggle: individual and hybrid impacts among double worker couples. Appl. Psychol. Int. Fire up. 66 628–652. 10.1111/apps.12103 [CrossRef] [Google Scholar]

33. Matthews W. S., Conger R. D., Wickrama K. A. S. (1996). Work-family strife and conjugal quality: intervening cycles. Soc. Psychol. Quart. 59 62–79. 10.2307/2787119 [CrossRef] [Google Scholar]

34. Michel J. S., Hargis B. (2008). Connecting systems of work-family struggle and division. J. Vocat. Behav. 73 509–522. 10.1016/j.jvb.2008.09.005 [CrossRef] [Google Scholar]

35. Plants M. J. ed. (2015). Sex and the Work-Family Experience: An Intersection of Two Domains. Cham: Springer; 10.1007/978-3-319-08891-4 [CrossRef] [Google Scholar]

36. Public Institute of Statistics (INE) (2018). Instituto Nacional de Estadística (INE) Survey. Accessible at: http://www.ine.es/ss/Satellite?L=es_ES&c=INE Seccion_C&cid=12 59950772779&p=1254735110672&pagename=ProductosYServicios%2F PYS Layout¶m1=PYSDetalle¶m3=1259924822888 [Google Scholar]

37. Nunnally H., Bernstein I. (1994). Psychometric Theory. New York, NY: McGraw-Hill. [Google Scholar]

38. Ogolsky B. G., Dennison R. P., Monk J. L. (2014). The function of couple inconsistencies in psychological and social populism in conjugal quality. Sex Roles 70 329–342. 10.1007/s11199-014-0365-9 [CrossRef] [Google Scholar]

39. Ollier-Malaterre A., Foucreault A. (2017). Cross-public work-life research: social and basic effects for people and associations. J. Oversee. 43 111–136. 10.1177/0149206316655873 [CrossRef] [Google Scholar]

40. Association for Economic Cooperation and Development [OECD] (2014). Adjusting Paid Work, Unpaid Work and Leisure. Accessible at: http://www.oecd.org/sex/information/balancing paid work unpaidworkandleisure.htm [Google Scholar]

41. Parsons T., Bales R. F. (1955). Family, Socialization and Interaction Process. Glencoe, IL: Free Press. [Google Scholar]

42. Paulin M., Lachance-Grzela M., McGee S. (2017). Bringing work home or carrying family to work: individual and social ramifications for working guardians. J. Fam. Econ. Issues 38 436–476. 10.1007/s10834-017-9524-9 [CrossRef] [Google Scholar]

43. Pitt-Catsouphes M., Kossek E. E., Sweet S. (2006). The Work and Family Handbook: Multi-Disciplinary Perspectives and Approaches. Mahwah, NJ: LEA. [Google Scholar]

44. Pittman J. F., Solheim C. A., Blandchard D. (1996). Stress as a driver of the allotment of familyShockley K. M., Shen W., DeNunzio M. M., Arvan M. L., Knudsen E. A. (2017). Unraveling the connection among sexual orientation and work-family strife: a joining of hypothetical viewpoints utilizing meta-scientific techniques. J. Appl. Psychol. 102 1601–1635. 10.1037/ap10000246 [PubMed] [CrossRef] [Google Scholar]

45. Sprung J. M., Toumbeva T. H., Matthews R. A. (2015). "Family-accommodating hierarchical strategies, practices, and advantages through the sex focal point," in Gender and the Work-Family Experience, ed. Factories M. (Cham: Springer;), 227–249. [Google Scholar]

46. Vinokur A. D., Van Ryn M. (1993). Social help and sabotaging in cozy connections: their free impacts on the emotional wellness of jobless people. J. Pers. Soc. Psychol. 65 350–359. 10.1037/0022-3514.65.2.350 [PubMed] [CrossRef] [Google Scholar]

47. Wayne J. H., Butts M. M., Casper W. J., Allen T. (2017). Looking for balance: an applied and experimental joining of various implications of work-family balance. Pers. Psychol. 70 167–210. 10.1111/peps.12132 [CrossRef] [Google Scholar]

48. Westman M., Etzion D. (2005). The hybrid of work-family strife from one life partner to the next. J. Appl. Soc. Psychol. 35 1936–1959. 10.1111/j.1559-1816.2005.tb02203.x [CrossRef] [Google Scholar]

49. Wharton A. S. (2015). (Un)Changing establishments: work, family and sexual orientation in the new economy. Sociol. Perspect. 58 7–19. 10.1177/0731121414564471 [CrossRef] [Google Scholar]

50. Wood W., Eagly A. H. (2010). "Sexual orientation," in Handbook of Social Psychology Vol. 1 fifth Edn, eds Fiske S. T., Gilbert D. T., Lindzey G. (Hoboken, NJ: John Wiley and Sons;), 629–667. [Google Scholar]

51. Yago C., Martínez M. C. (2009). "La distribución del trabajo doméstico y la percepción de injusticia en las mujeres (Domestic work dissemination and shamefulness discernment in ladies)," in Género y Conciliación de la Vida Familiar y Laboral un Análisis Psicosocial (Gender and Work-Family Conciliation: A Psychodocial Analysis), ed. Martínez M. C. (Murcia: Servicio de Publicaciones Universidad de Murcia;), 125–142. [Google Scholar]

7

Government Initiatives Towards Empowerment of Rural Women in India: A Conceptual Study

Dr. Shivi Mittal[1]

Bhavana Sharma[2]

Nishant Singh[2]

1. Department of Management Studies, G.L Bajaj Institute of Technology & Management , A.P.J Abdul Kalam Technical University, Gautam Buddha Nagar, 201306, India.
2. Department of Management Studies, G.L Bajaj Institute of Management &Research, A.P.J Abdul Kalam Technical University, Gautam Buddha Nagar, 201306, India.

Abstract: Women empowerment and up gradation in rural India is one of the most crucial and burning issues which needs attention and consideration to reach the goal of "Power to Empower". Rural society in India is continuously hesitant towards the women in providing support related to work, decisions matter, mobility etc, and even they didn't get support from their family as well as from their spouse. The main objective of this paper is to examine the initiatives taken by the government and policies and schemes framed by the Financial institute for empowering women and raising their status and standard of living. Various challenges and obstacles faced by women in rural India is also being highlighted in this paper. A conceptual study is done and several clients' stories are also discussed to give a boost to the paper.

In the end, we find that in spite of various support initiated by government and financial institutions, women are still facing many challenges and obstacles which need to be rid off. And only women have that power and courage with which they can "empower" themselves. Last but not least India should reach that level which empowers not only women but the whole human society, "Power to Empower".

Keywords: Women empowerment, rural women, Government policies, Self-Help Groups

1. INTRODUCTION

1.1 WOMEN EMPOWERMENT

Women's strengthening is the most key framework to reinforce the eventual fate of women in India. It is an orderly approach which needs to grow all the more genuinely in India. The Government of India came up in the new thousand years by announcing the year 2001 as Women's Empowerment Year' to concentrate on a dream 'where women are equivalent accomplices like men'. Women are turning out to be progressively hesitant about their segregation in a few ranges of family and open life. Strengthening would turn out to be more applicable if they are instructed, better educated and can take balanced choices.

Strengthening is a theoretical and complex idea and it is deciphered from various perspectives. Strengthening originates from the term engage which signifies "to give power or power" and "to empower to allow". The key components in strengthening are "empowering" and 'giving force'. Also, they strengthen one another. As such, strengthening would mean the procedure of testing existing disparity, Power relations, and of increasing more noteworthy control over wellsprings of force by the under-advantaged.

Sexual orientation fairness and women strengthening are critical components for the social and financial advancement of a country. The advancement of sex uniformity and women strengthening is one of the Eight Millennium Development Goals (MDG) to which India is a signatory, yet to date, no real endeavours have been made to build up a thorough system for measuring and following changes in the levels of strengthening. Women strengthening is conceptualized as a component of ladies' entrance to and control over assets, which reaches out to their choice settling on abilities with respect to family unit choices, occupation, salary, family unit resources and use and opportunity of development i.e. physical versatility and their control over material and immaterial assets, for example, property, data and time, their position inside of the family unit and so forth.

1.2 ROLE OF MICROFINANCE IN WOMEN EMPOWERMENT

Microfinance programs have been progressively advanced in India for their positive financial effect and the conviction that they enable women. Women's strengthening is a procedure in which women challenge the current standards and society, to viably enhance their prosperity. Most microfinance projects target women with the unequivocal objective of engaging them. Then again, their basic premises are distinctive. Some contend that women are amongst the poorest and the most powerless of the underprivileged. Others trust that putting resources into women' abilities enables them to settle on decisions, which will add to more noteworthy financial development and advancement. At last, a few defenders underline that an expansion in lady's assets results in higher prosperity of the family, particularly youngsters. Small scale money programs for ladies have been advanced throughout the years as a system for neediness mitigation as well as for women strengthening. There has been an outlook change from microfinance and pay era to a more incorporated way to deal with engage women. Country women have numerous parts and obligations. They are agriculturists, guardians, wage workers and smaller scale business visionaries and they frequently spend numerous hours getting water and gathering kindling. The strengthening of women is principal to decrease destitution, craving and ailing health.

1.3 DO SELF-HELP GROUPS REALLY HELP WOMEN TO EMPOWER?

Self Help Groups are clusters of about 10 to 20 individuals who come forward with a purpose of exterminating poverty and social change through their own involvement. They provide low interest loans to the followers after a large sum has been shared. First of all, a group is formed, then all the members contribute some capital and then they are involved in economic events. SHGs are sometimes also referred to as "Micro banks" which have funds either of their own or through some other involvement of associations, cooperatives, MFIs and banks. They are the direct link to the poor people and hence the microfinance segment advances around them. They are either associated with the banks or to the MFIs.

2. CHALLENGES AND OBSTACLES FACED BY RURAL WOMEN IN INDIA

1. Support from family: Rural women often found less support from their family members.As per their traditional mindset, women are not allowed to go for work. They are only restricted to the household chores and looking after the kids. If any woman go out for work and earn, societal issues may create which led to the family members to prohibit their woman to go out from homes.

2. Knowledge and awareness: In spite of several awareness programmes offered by the government from time to time, women are found less aware and knowledgeable related to their empowerment. For this, there are a number of reasons like less support from family members, societal issues etc.

3. Male dominance and Gender discrimination: In developing country like India, women are still leading by males whether they are from urban or rural India. Male's decisions are given crucial importance over females. Decisions related to matters like from social, domestic, financial as well as

their empowerment is being decided by their husbands or male members in the family.

4. Finance: Another problem faced by rural women in India is that they don't have finance for starting or managing their business, they also don't get any significant financial support from their family and due to lack of knowledge and awareness about the policies related to development of women entrepreneurs and entrepreneurship, they are not able to start or manage their business . Many banks do not find rural women good applicants to provide loans also.

5. Legal formability: In India female entrepreneurs find problems in comprehending legal formalities and due to this they are not able to understand and follow the legal constraints and procedure regarding starting and maintaining the venture.

6. Balance between work and family: As India is male ruling society, taking care of the home, family and youngsters are as yet the duty of the female individual from the family, because of this they invest heaps of their energy satisfying these duties and find less an ideal opportunity to zero in on the business. With no support from the others members of family women find no time for themselves and for their career and development.

7. Social cultural Barrier: In India women are still perceived as the weaker, less knowledgeable and less skillful in comparison to the men. Still women in India are not able to make their own decision. In rural areas females are perceived as only capable of handling household chores and not able to understand the complexity of the outer world. If any woman go out for work and earn, societal issues may arise which led to the family members to prohibit their woman to go out from homes.

8. Risk bearing capability: Women are found to have less risk bearing capability while doing work etc. They are often termed as 'Bechari'. Due to lack of knowledge, awareness,

confidence and moral support from family members, they find themselves less capable of taking risk in business.

9. Competition: Rural women entrepreneurs also faced stiff competition in the market as business still is male dominated. They are also scared of starting tiny vemtures.

10. Transportation and Mobility for Female : In India many places are not safe for women. Even going in these kinds of places even females also want support from their male friends or male family members.

11. Arrangement of finance in all stages of business: Another problem faced by rural women entrepreneurs is that they are not able to find the sources of finance to maintain the business in later stages.

12. Lack of knowledge about concession and scheme: Due to lack of knowledge about concession and scheme women entrepreneurs are not able to get benefits of it in spite of many efforts from the government and other financial institutions.

13. Traditional mindset: India is male dominating society although women are working but still due to traditional mindset they need to take permission from their family. Due male dominating society women are still not treated as male gender and face many restrictions in the family as well as in the society.

14. Self Confidence: Next problem faced by women is lack of self confidence as they get upset very easily due to lack of support and nurturing environment. Self doubt and insecurities make it worse.

15. Raw material availability: Many female entrepreneurs faced the problem of availability of raw material also. As due to lack of knowledge they are not able to find material as well as a market where they can find raw material at a low or discounted price and are not able to find the alternative material also.

16. Lack of networks: Many rural entrepreneur women of India are not able to develop networks which can help them or

can provide guidance to them. Many females are not able to find a mentor in their journey who can guide them and help them to Manage their ventures. Networking also helps them to identify new procedures, trends and technologies to enhance their skills and knowledge and working capabilities.

17. Middle man and skillful employees : Due to lack of network or resources female entrepreneurs in india are not able to find the middle man and skillful employee to work with. As India is male dominated society, many male do not want to work under the female leader and does not provide support them

18. Difficulty in finding the right customer: Next Problem faced by Indian rural entrepreneurs is that they are not able to find the right market or customer for their products or services in spite of getting training from several Entrepreneurs development programmes. Due to lack of support from mentors or guidance , most of the time they choose the wrong market or customer to target.

19. I nterference of Family: In India women are still powerless and incapable of taking their own decision , from their education to marriage all decisions were taken by their families. if somehow female start their own venture then also their family member takes unnecessary interest in their business and put lot of pressure of completing household chores or taking care of children

20. Caste discrimination: Caste discrimination is a big issue in India. Due to this one caste only supports same caste entrepreneurs and does not provide support to other castes. Female entrepreneurs also face the same kind of problem, Some castes can boycott their product or services.If female entrepreneurs belong to lower caste then upper caste people will never purchase their product or services because they feel and think that lower class people are not clean or pure as they are.

3. GOVERNMENT INITIATIVES AND POLICIES FRAMED

1. Mahila Udyam Nidhi Scheme: This policy is obtainable by one of the old and reliable banks that is Punjab National Bank in association with the Small Industries Development Bank of India. This policy helps Women to open their small-scale business and provide loans unto ten Lakh Rupees and 3-5 years for repayment and also an additional 5 years conjointly. the rate of interest depends upon the market rate accessible at that specific time. This policy also provides different plans for a different business like daycare, beauty parlor, etc. This Scheme also supports female entrepreneurs to upgrade their business also.

2. Cent Kalyani Scheme:The second theme in this criterion is Cent Kalyani Scheme. This scheme mainly focuses on business which is related to the manufacturing and services sectors. This Scheme is provided by the Central Bank of India and provides support to new as well as existing micro and small scale businesses. Under this Scheme women, entrepreneurs can get loans up to a huge amount of one Crore with a margin of 20 percent. The rate of interest for loan rupees up to 10 lakhs is 7.85% and the interest rate above 10 lakh to one crore is 8.10%. Some of the important aspects of this scheme are that there are no processing fees, no third party and Collateral security required and optional insurance is also available.

3. Stree Shakti Package for Women Entrepreneurs: This package is provided by the State bank of India which helps women entrepreneurs and supports them by providing some types of concessions. This scheme mainly helps women who have majority ownership mean more than 50 percent of stake in the business. If women entrepreneurs want to take support from this policy, they have to enroll themselves in the Entrepreneurship Development Programmed which is supported or organized by a state agency. In this, up to 5 lakh rupees loans are provided without any security for MSME. This Scheme provides a loan of more than 2 lakh rupees with a concession of 0.05 percent.

4. Annapurna Scheme: This Scheme is provided by the Government of India and especially provides support to women entrepreneurs to start their business especially in the food catering business and grant loans up to 50000 rupees. After sanctioned loan taker can repay the loan amount in 36 months which includes no EMI For the first month. The interest rate is based on market conditions. For this scheme, a guarantor is important for applying or availing the loans and other assets for the venture. Women entrepreneurs can use their loan amount as working capital and can buy cutlery, utensils, and other catering-related products.

5. Bharatiya Mahila Bank (BMB) business loan: This bank provides loans up to 20 crores for Manufacturing at the interest rate of 10.15% and up to 1 crore for collateral-free loans for MSME under the Credit Guarantee Funds Trust and repayment for this loan should be completed in 7 years. This Bank is part of the State Bank of India since 1 April 2017. BMB provides mainly four Scheme:

- Shringaar- BeautyParlour/Saloon/Spa
- Annapurna Food Catering
- SME Easy - Small and Medium Enterprises
- Parvarish- Day Care Centre

6) **Dena Shakti scheme:** This loan facility is provided by the bank of Baroda to women entrepreneurs which want to start their business to education, housing and retail & small business enterprises, microcredit education, and agriculture. There is also a concession in the rate of interest of 0.25%. As per the direction of RBI, this scheme provides 20 lakh loan up to for the retail sector as well as for education and housing and 50 thousand for microcredit.

7. **Orient Mahila Vikas Yojana scheme:** This scheme is launched by the Oriental Bank of Commerce. It basically gives support by providing capital to aspiring women to

start their venture. For this loan, women must have more than 51 % share in the business. The loan amount between 10 lakhs to 25 lakhs required no collateral, especially for small-scale industry. It also offers a concession of 2% on the rate of interest and the repayment period is 7 years long.

8) **Udyogini scheme:** This scheme is provided by Punjab and Sind Bank and Kerala State Women's Development Corporation. For applying for this loan applicants need to be a woman and must have age between 18 to 55 years and the family income should be not more than 1.5 lakh. If a woman applicant belongs to special categories like the widow, SC/ST, and disabled then there is no upper limit of income required. The maximum amount of the loan is up to 3 lakhs. This scheme also helps in imparting skills related to planning, pricing, costing, etc. The government also provided a 30% subsidy on loans extended. This loan is also free from collateral.

4. CASE STUDIES

1. CLIENT STORIES

- **Tailoring shop set with loan ensures steady income to the client:** A person named Rajendra from a dalit family, borrowed a loan from Disha MFI and started a small tailoring shop . This initiative marked a new beginning for him. His business has started picking up and this has facilitated him to pay regularly.
- **Finance helps the family set up a paper plate unit:** A SHG heralded a ray of hope in the life of Santosh who joined "Vikas SHG". She takes a loan and start a business of paper plates which increased her standard of living.
- **Loan enables family to start a new venture:** Anita from a dalit family become a member of "Khushboo SHG" and start a new venture of repair parts of electrical appliances with her husband. This has raised her family standard of living.

- **Financial support causes income to rise:**Another woman with the help of loan taken by SHG has started a business of tailoring which causes her income to rise.

4. CONCLUSIONS AND RECOMMENDATIONS

In this paper, while studying we come across many problems faced by rural women in India such as lack of knowledge, awareness, support, finance etc. In Spite of various policies framed and initiatives taken by many financial institutions, women are found less aware and capable.

They need all that guidance and support which a man gets from society. All the issues and challenges are being faced by women but a man gets financial, societal and family support from the members as well.

The question arises who needs to empower? Our society as a whole or a woman? A woman who gives birth to a life needs to empower? Really? If yes, then in what sense?

Still, women are facing that male dominance which is a main barrier to our Indian culture. Our suggestion is that such campaigns need to be held in future so that the very purpose will be solved. The benefits of such will actually reach to these needy clans for whom it is made.

BIBLIOGRAPHY

- Rajkhowa.,M. " Problem Faced by Rural Women Entrepreneurs in the Dibrugarh District of Assam." Journal of Interdisciplinary Cycle Research, Volume XII, Issue VI, June/2020, Page No:474,ISSN NO: 0022-1945.
- Singh.,H. "Empowerment of Women: A sociological study of Malwa region of punjab". Alochana Chakra Journal, Volume IX, Issue V, May/2020 Page No:4323.
- Chatterjee,S.,Gupta S.D.,Upadhyay,P. "Technology adoption and entrepreneurial orientation for rural women: Evidence from India". Technological Forecasting and Social Change., Volume 160, November2020.https://doi.org/10.1016/j.techfore.2020.120236.
- Mandhyan,P. Parth,K., "Women Empowerment Realities and Challenges". Splint International Journal of Professionals: A

Quarterly Peer Reviewed Multi-Disciplinary International Journal; Bhubaneswar Vol. 7, Iss. 2, (Apr-Jun 2020): 55-58.

- Smriti,R., " Multi-Dimensional Approach for Women Empowerment." . International Journal of Research and Analytical Reviews, September 2020, Volume 7, Issue 3.E-ISSN 2348-1269, P-ISSN 2349-5138.
- Shukla.M., " Women Empowerment as Agency Expansion." EPRA International Journal of Research and Development (IJRD)Volume: 5 | Issue: 10 | October 2020 - Peer Reviewed JournalSJIF Impact Factor: 7.001 | ISI I.F.Value:1.241 | Journal DOI: 10.36713/epra2016 ISSN: 2455-7838(Online)
- Yoopetch, C. (2020), "Women empowerment, attitude toward risk-taking and entrepreneurial intention in the hospitality industry", International Journal of Culture, Tourism and Hospitality Research, Vol. ahead-of-print No. ahead-of-print.https://doi.org/10.1108/IJCTHR-01-2020-0016
- Vijayakumar., N. "Challenges and Prospects of Micro Women Entrepreneurs in Tiruvallur District of Tamilnadu". Emperor Journal of Economics and Social Science Research Vol-V, issue 11, November 2019, ISSN: 2581-8643(O).

Ï% Pathak, P. "Women Empowerment and Self Help Groups in India." Asian Journal of Research in Social Sciences and Humanities 8 (5), 15-20, 2018

- Pathak.A., Varshney,S."Challenges faced by women entrepreneurs in rural India: The case of Avika".The International Journal of Entrepreneurship and Innovation 18 (1), 65-72, 2017.
- Sharma, A.,Dua,S., Hatwal.V., "Micro Enterprise Development and Rural Women Entrepreneurship: Way for Economic Empowerment:" Arth Prabhand: A Journal of Economics and Management Vol.1 Issue 6, September 2012, ISSN 2278 0629.
- Kumari.S,Kaushik.V., Lodha.N., "ProblemFaced by Rural Women Entrepreneurs of Rajasthan",Stud Home Comm Sci, 4(2): 115-119 (2010).
- https://www.bajajfinserv.in/udyogini-scheme
- https://www.paisabazaar.com/business-loan/udyogini-scheme/

8

Gender Equality: Why it should be a Matter to Discuss?

Dr. Preeti Pal

Department of Biotechnology, Institute of Applied Science and Humanities, GLA University, Mathura, India. 281406

Abstract: Gender inequality has been a social issue not only in India but all over the world for centuries. In many parts of India, the birth of a girl child is not welcomed as the birth of boy child. It is not even matter of hiding that discrimination starts right from their birth at their own home. There have been ennemerous cases of killing of girl child in the foetus itself. No wonder which makes the child sex ratio of 1000 boys over 898 girls. There are several strong steps have been taken by the government through releasing slogans and posters for saving girl child and education girl child in India. Schemes have been implemented increase the awareness in the society for educating girl child.

Patriarchal norms since ages have marked women as inferior to men. It is very well set in the society that a girl child is considered as a burden and is often not even allowed to lead her life as she wants. She has to live under many false rules and regulations which are evidently not anywhere in the law system. Despite such discrimination in education, health, protection or participation in this male dominated world, women have proved to be strong leaders in every field possible.

1. Introduction

Gender equality, the word carries the same weight as the women carrying the burden of injustice since ages. Though gender equality and women empowerment terms are being widely used in recent years, the results seems invisible as of now. A handful of people are working hard in this direction to achieve gender equality and to empower women and girls.

Why it should be the matter to discuss?

In my opinion, when the child takes birth he/she doesn't know that what will be his/her right and what he/she will face after few years. But as soon as he/she enters this world, parents distinguish them. Parents or grandparents see them as a boy who will be the in-charge of property and a girl who will take care of household chores because she has to marry somebody. Most importantly, they don't even know that they are discriminating. In their mind it is already set that, this is perfectly fine to discriminate. Their belief is so rigid that our education system also fails to change this mentality.

It should not be a matter to discuss because we all are human beings and this mother earth and all resources are equally available for each and every human being. On the other hand, we have created a lot of fuss on this beautiful earth where every animal, bird, insect, plants, trees, male female, everybody has been given their role to play. But somehow human beings have evolved thinking that male is superior to female and hence there should not be equal right for both. After centuries of negligence, violence, a handful of intelligent people have given a thought that there is something wrong with the society.

About half of the world's population and world's potential are women and girls. Gender inequality persists in almost every part of the world which ultimately limited the growth of the women in every field. Women's and girls' education and their empowerment is vital for expanding economic growth and promoting social development [1].

2. Inequality at home

It is well known fact that women face every kind of discrimination at home and in a normal middle class family or lower middle class family any girl grow up with the feeling of inferiority. Often they are victim of domestic violence. Apart from education, there are a number of other factors which are interconnected and responsible for the prevalence of gender inequality. One of the root cause is of gender inequality in Indian society lies in its patriarchal system. The system which allows men to hold the authority over female family members. They also inherit family property and title. It is reported that, 1 in 5 women and girls between the ages of 15 and 49 report experiencing physical or sexual violence by an intimate partner within a 12-month period [2].

The middle class is most gender conservative and especially in Indian society is patriarchal. In our society only male persons take the decisions on behalf of all family members. The decision of children's education, marriage, and job mostly taken by their families. The low female literacy rate has had a dramatically negative impact on family planning and population stabilisation efforts. Uneducated mothers are not aware of the best nutritional choices for their children. Though this trend is changing slowly, the condition of girls and women in most part of India is almost same. Even the upper middle class families and rich people they do not want their daughters to do any job. The reason being they have enough money and they don't want their girl to be in any kind of job for others. Parents are responsible for limiting educational opportunities. In the last two decades, educational and professional opportunities for women have increased up to a certain level but not as much as it is required.

3. Inequality in education system:

Start from home male child has been given priority in each and every aspect of life whether it is in toys, education, property or any other thing they want in their life. Generally it happens in families that education is very limited for girls. Parents want their son to be educated in a quality institute while for girl child the wont spend much money. The thinking persist in the mind that, there will be safety issues, besides they girl has to get married and will be going to other's hose so after that it is their responsibility whether they want her to do job or not.

The condition of girls is like they can never make decisions of their own. Before marriage, its parents decision for her, after marriage in laws and husband is solely responsible for taking decisions on her behalf. That is disheartening to see but it will take at least more than a century to change.

Uneducated families are less likely to send their own children to school because they do not want to spend money on education as they may think it is not much important. Without quality education, women lack confidence and knowledge about their rights which prevent them to make their own choice and are encouraged or forced to marry early. India holds the miserable record of having the highest absolute number of child brides: about 24 million. This represents 40% of the world's 60 million child marriages [3]. Because of early marriage, girls gain adulthood and motherhood before they even know what their life is about. They have to suffer a lot when they are not emotionally or physically mature. This not only affects girls' life but the next generation also suffers because of lack of knowledge and education in the parents. Less educated girls unable to understand the value of the involvement in the family and they don't realise the unequal power relations, which ultimately are less likely to contribute for the nations' economy.

4. Inequality in private and government jobs

The full participation of women in ever field of job and entrepreneurship, will led to the improvement of economy of a country. Due to the inequality in recruiting the male and female candidates in the government and private organisations and also societal thinking of not seeing girls/women as an independent person created a gap. Gupta (2017) very well explained with the survey that how the growth and development of a female affected due to inequality and the staying late in office culture [3]. Preferring hiring male candidates over female candidates are also very common in every sector of job. The reason for this partiality is somewhere that, females can not stay after office hours, which is accepted a sign of had worker in especially corporate fields. Also there are other constraints such as marriage issues, maternity leaves, other family, children's issue related leaves. Because in every family, lower, upper or middle class, females have to manage so many things together. Which might sometimes affect their work at office?

5. Gender equality and sustainable growth

There are several steps taken to eradicate the gender inequality from India and improve the situation of girls. There are measures taken by the government to increase the girl sex ration and increasing the percentage of girls in schools, colleges and government jobs. The Government of India, along with various states, initiated various policies, programmes and schemes intended to reduce the gender inequality and to boost women's empowerment over the 1989-2015 period. Some of them are Swa-Shakthi, Swawlamban programme, Indira Gandhi Matritva Sahyog Yojana Conditional Maternity Benefit plan (IGMSY-CMB), Support to Training and Employment Programme for Women, Swawalamban Programme, Swashakti Project, Integrated Child Development Services, Indira Mahila Yojana (IMY), Maliha Samridhi Yojana (MSY), Balika Samriddhi Yojana (BSY), National Programme of

Nutritional Support to Primary Education, National Programme for Education of Girls at Elementary Level, Sukyana, Ladli Laxmi Yojana, Apni Beti-Apna Dhan (ABAD) and many more. It is also illegal to know the gender of the child through diagnostic techniques under Pre-Conception and Pre-Natal Diagnostic Techniques Act, 1994. Many slogans are circulated by government to inspire the audiences to spread awareness about educating a girl child for the empowerment of family, society and the nation as well [4]. All the above mentioned schemes if implemented properly there would be a definite change in the society.

6. Conclusions

In-spite of efforts doing for fighting gender inequality, unfortunately, girl child is not being treated well in our society. We have to raise our voice for them. Gender equality is not only a fundamental human right, but a necessary foundation for a peaceful, prosperous and sustainable world. Educate each girl child and brightens the future of country. Educate each girl child to promote the weak section of the society and to improve the generations of family. Educating and empowering a girl child is the best way to improve the family, society, and a nation. It emphasizes the need for coordinated and integrated policy responses, implementing existing legislation, and ensuring greater accountability from governments in order to eliminate this violence. There are already a number of schemes available which are really good for empowering the conditions of girls or women in the villages. All the schemes should be implemented and monitored correctly to see the change in the society. We should take steps on individual level to spread awareness regarding the government schemes so that children should get benefitted from them.

References

1. https://www.un.org/sustainabledevelopment/wp-content/uploads/2016/08/5_Why-It-Matters-2020.pdf
2. https://www.un.org/sustainabledevelopment/gender-equality/
3. Namrata Gupta, 2017, Gender inequality in the work environment: a study of private research organizations in India. (www.emeraldinsight.com/2040-7149.htm)
4. Singh Sumanjeet, 2017, The state of gender inequality in india. (DOI: 10.1515/genst-2017-0009).

9

Empowered Women, Empower Women

Dr. Seema Negi

Global Goodwill Ambassador
Principal, Sanjeevani World School
Life coach, Eduleader

Behind every successful woman is a tribe of other successful women who have her back!

How would you define empowerment? What does empowerment mean to you? Were you ever subdued and were you ever left feeling incapacitated? If your answer was yes for just one question, it could perhaps be because instead of someone holding your hand to lift you up, you were only repressed.

This could be a feeling most women could feel and that's unfortunately is a common trademark in most of the establishments be it a corporate firm or an educational institute. A feature that is unnoticed in most places of work, or even a home set up per se. There is a substratum of truth that women are the cause for a stumbling block for progression in women. So, when the foundations of Sanjeevani World School were laid, when it was at its primitive phase, at the inception, we were determined to break this stereotype and weave a different narrative.

'When women support each other, incredible things happen.' This was the kind of culture we worked upon at the onset of the gestation period. The vision or the aim of our work culture was to promote or facilitate an environment where all women feel appreciated, that they are important and that they know their worth. It is when women are ignored or when their inner potential or caliber is not recognized or tapped, inferiority seeps in. There's a sense of vacuum created which does not let you be happy and that in turn stops you from seeing others happy.

In our school we promote growth. 'You can always tell who the strong women are. They are the ones building one another up rather than tearing each another down.' We not only ensure we make every woman feel important but also help them now their own work. Hence for us this line is apt and comes easily: 'Celebrate her success without questioning your own.' Here is a recipe of an empowered woman where

- W stands for Willingness: Willingness to promote equal opportunities for growth.
- O stands for Optimistic: Be optimistic to see new prospects; learn from different situations and move forward.
- M stands for Master: Master the art of balancing emotions to be professional.
- A stands for Attitude: Have an attitude of 'We' not 'I' because 'I' leads to illness and 'W' leads to wellness.
- N – Noble character: Nobility comes with inner beauty and not outwardly. Work towards beautifying inner self. It is a royal virtue, so be the queen that others would admire and wish to model.

Women empowerment, a term that all of us are extremely familiar with in the 21st century. But what does it mean exactly? And why is it such a prevalent topic day in and day out?

Well the answer is quite simple, with the changing times come the changing tides, where women are slowly coming into their power and reaching their full potential everywhere. They are demanding their equal rights and scouting out opportunities that rival men which would not have been possible just a few decades ago. Whether it be financially, politically, culturally or emotionally, women are regaining their independence bit by bit as observed in the past couple years. Through the decades we have noticed how the wheel has turned and how the opportunities given to women have been increasing in every sector each passing day.

This is encouraged by our government as well, the "Beti Bachao, Beti Padhao", campaign putting emphasis on the absolute importance of education which is the first step to empowerment. Through education young girls learn about their rights and responsibilities and how they can achieve every goal they dream of without having to fret over the glass ceiling, breaking the glass ceiling is a feat that more and more women are able to experience with the newer standards of what defines womanhood.

Where it once meant that women were treated as a liability and property with little to no freedom or rights, we now see them owning property, being at the top of the corporate world standing tall besides men. Even though there are only a few for now, down the line we will be able to see more of them with the progression of society.

Let us see where it all started, and slightly go back in time. Savitribai Phule, a name that has been used as motivation for women for years, helping them believe that even through the harshness and prejudice of society, if you want something nothing can stop you from reaching your goal. In 1848 AD, Savitribai Phule was the first female educator in India, this was the start of something that would break societal norms for years to come. Then, in 1985 the concept of women empowerment was introduced at the UN's Third World Conference on Women in Nairobi, which defined it as a redistribution of social and economic powers and control of resources in favor of women. Even still, it was a long time before women felt true liberation and freedom. A century after Savitribai Phule paved a rough path for women, India got its first female prime minister, Indira Gandhi who changed the political landscape for the better.

Females are breaking all the stereotypes and proving their mettle in diverse fields. For a visionary society to thrive, it's imperative to maintain gender equality in all arenas social, economic, political.

To conclude; she overcame everything that was meant to destroy her, she is a woman, she is power, she is peace, she is the one capable of making impossible - I M possible, all she needs is equal opportunity.

Lift, build and uphold one another, with this thought how befitting it is for one sect of the community to uplift the other, the current pandemic has taught us resilience, perseverance and has reminded mankind once again to be empathetic.

10

Feminism: Genesis and Progression

Dr. Honey Singhal

Senior Content Writer,
Dentalkart, VASA Denticity Pvt. Ltd., New Delhi.

Dr. Hitesh Gupta

Chairman and Editor-in-Chief
SPEAK Foundation, Delhi.

Abstract: A movement named feminism, also evolved and named as post-feminism, also misunderstood and got named as pseudo feminism, has evolved and gained enormous familiarity in the masses. Terms like 'sexism', 'sexist oppression' 'women liberation', 'gender equality', 'girl power' are no more only found in texts but it is known and understood by common people due to its acceleration at global level. Its flame is now bright and well established among mob, it would also have its own challenges and consequences like any other doctrine; therefore, it is important to understand its origin and about the forerunners who laid its foundation. In this continuous process of considering the subject of how and why sexual roles differ, there seems to be an evident backlash which is prominently present in all aspects of male female relationships. The feminist ideology gave rise to arguments searching for reasons lying at the core of all the issues. Man's control over women's sexuality created hostile surroundings which lead to oppressed feminine nature. This chapter will discuss women's stance beginning from Greek mythologies, Shakespearean women, ideologies of feminist precursors like Mary Wollstonecraft and Virginia Woolf, three waves of feminism and feminism in Indian context. As it is always wise to understand a theory from its origin, this chapter envisages how feminism evolved as a nomenclature and a distinct and indispensable branch of contemporary literature.

Keywords: women, feminism, equality, liberation, patriarchy

INTRODUCTION

The meaning of feminism has been deconstructed several times and is still contradictory. A French novelist and Philosopher Simone de Beauvoir, in her book *The Second Sex* said, "One is not born, but rather becomes, a woman"[1], which propelled many minds and instigated the wave of feminism. Feminism is a way which endeavours to analyse literature from the point of view of a woman. How does she view and observe objects around her; how she makes an effort to analyse different things which justify her ego in a medium which is dissimilar from the expression of menfolk. Feminism is woman's sense of reaction against man's dominance in social, political, economic fields of life. It is all about a vehement advocacy for establishment of their individuality and rights, denied so extensively by the male control. This can be termed as a woman's genuine craving, very well reflected in the works of art and literature as well. Prominent feminist literature began in the last decade of eighteenth century when Mary Wollstonecraft wrote *A Vindication of the Rights of Woman* in 1792. Ever since then feminist writers are writing to struggle for woman's liberty and equality. Feminist canon of literature emerged first in the Western countries and eventually found place in developing countries too.

> "A feminist is anyone who recognizes the equality and full humanity of women and men."[2] - Gloria Steinem

General and varied perception of feminism is now already well-established. Although it's a common and currently infamous term, people seem to have formed their own customized derivations of feminism based on their environment, exposure and thought process. Since the wave of feminism is catching higher magnitude in contemporary literature, it has expanded into a vast and diverse genre with varied complexities and comprehensions.

Coming to the definition of feminism several authors and poets have tried to define feminism in different ways a few commonly accepted and known definitions would be: A British comedic writer Caitlin Moran when asked as to what feminism is, replied, "Simply the belief that women should be as free as men, however nuts, dim, deluded, badly dressed, fat, receding, lazy and smug they might be."[3] An Australian contemporary feminist writer G.D. Anderson wrote in her essay, that "Feminism isn't about making women stronger, women are already strong, it's about changing the way the world perceives that strength"[4].

When one tries to find how ancient literature pieces experienced difference between men and women, we find traces of feminism inherent in there. Aristotle's (384-322 BC) critical idea in early fourth century BC was that, "women were women by virtue of a certain lack of qualities"[5]. He argued that women are inferior to men by nature and must therefore be subordinate to, and ruled by men. He laid his judgment based on biological differences and concluded that woman "is as it were a deformed male"[6]. As per him, woman's inability to produce semen was the only active principle, which got conceptualized and got accepted in the West for at least fifteen centuries. However, this ideology is not given much weightage today as he considered only physical and mental attributes.

The renaissance period of literature was dominated by Shakespearean plays which projected women as rather complex beings in action and not always subdued or shadowed behind others' psyche and decisions. Already set notions need to first deconstruct to reassess and analyze whether Shakespeare's women were strong or weak. Characters built by Shakespeare were never one-dimensional, they were rather complex and layered, carried both positive and negative orientation.

Europe experienced the flame of feminism in the eighteenth century when the two philosophers Voltaire in France and John Locke in England gave the ideals of dignity, equality, and liberty for all. A silent tradition which was running in an opposite flow to the ideals given was deeply incorporated in the minds of people and did not let women wonder upon if they had any rights to even dream of a life beyond the set boundaries.

It is essential to understand patriarchy to be able to see the gender-based hierarchy seen throughout the globe. Patriarchal structure runs in a way that governs descent of a family name and heritage only via male members of the family and thereby women are clearly excluded. This social system which led to suppression and inequality towards women became the prominent cause of male dominance and other countereffects.

BEGINNING OF FEMINIST LITERATURE

Widely accepted literary text which is believed until today to have begun the feminist writings is a manifesto 'A Vindication of the Rights of Woman' (1792) written by a British philosopher Mary Wollstonecraft (1759-1797). She argued that women were as wise and deserving as men and hence are worthy of similar dignity and respect. Identifying that biology is not one's destiny, she said, "I view, with indignation, the mistaken notions that enslave my sex"[7]. In her opening lines of 'A Vindication of the Rights of Woman', she expressed her "profound conviction that the neglected education of (women) is the grand source of the misery I deplore"[7]. She advised that "strengthen the female mind by enlarging it, and there will be an end to blind obedience"[7].

Another prominent feminist writer known after Mary Wollstonecraft is Virginia Woolf (1882 - 1942). She delivered a lecture at Cambridge University which was also later released as an essay called 'A Room of One's Own'. The title of the essay is a summarized notion from Woolf's conception that, "a woman must have money and a room of her own if she is to write fiction"[8]. Woolf noted that poverty and lack of financial freedom were two major obstacles which kept women away from writing what they feel.

UNDERSTANDING THREE WAVES OF FEMINISM

Feminism has been broadly divided into three phases termed as three waves of feminism. The first wave, beginning in the mid-nineteenth century till early twentieth century; the second wave in the 1960s and 1970s; while third wave started in 1990s and continues till present.

The First Wave

The first wave feminists included Abigail Adams, Mary Wollstonecraft, Angelina Grimke, Lucretia Matt, Elizabeth Cady Stanton, Harriet Taylor Mill, Caroline Norton and John Stuart Mill. The first wave feminism focused majorly on suffrage campaigns and fight against legal obstacles towards gender equality. Achievements of first wave feminists were: the opening of higher education to women and enactment of the Married Women's Property Act (1870).

First wave feminism is commonly referred to the feminist activities which evolved in the second half of the 19th century in the USA and Britain. This movement challenged women's lack of access to education, contract and property rights against women, unequal employment opportunities, marriage laws etc.

Abigail Adams (1744-1818) was the wife of John Adams, the second president of the USA. She regularly urged her husband to 'remember to think about the Ladies' while drafting the Declaration of Independence. She warned, "If particular care and attention is not paid to the ladies, we are determined to foment a rebellion, and will not hold ourselves bound by any laws which we have no voice, or representation"[9]. She demanded equal representation within the law and also reminded against lack of access to education. Since she was away from her husband when the Declaration was planned, she expressed her ideas and suggestions via letters. These letters were later compiled and published posthumously by her grandson. She asserted, "If we mean to have heroes, statesmen, and philosophers, we should have learned women"[10].

Jean Jacques Rousseau (1712-78), a Swiss-French philosopher claimed that women are sentimental and frivolous in his book 'Emile'. He believed that women could occupy their position as companions to their men and was completely untroubled by the subordination of women. Wollstonecraft, who was earlier an admirer of Rousseau, was altogether disturbed by his claims and wrote 'A Vindication of the Rights of Woman' as an answer to his book. As a liberal feminist, she believed in the freedom of speech to women and concluded that independent and rational women develop better moral capacities and therefore become 'observant daughters', 'affectionate sisters', 'reasonable mothers' and 'faithful wives'.

Sisters Sarah Grimke and Angelina Grimke (Grimke Sisters) were born in South Carolina into a slave-holding family. They were orators, writers, educators and Quakers who were first American women to fight for women's rights. Sarah Grimke published 'Letters on the Equality of the Sexes' had developed sentiments against slavery and subordination of women. Angelina Grimke, in a lecture in public, in 1838, notified the female audience that, "Men who hold the rod over slaves, rule in the councils of the nation: and they deny our right to petition and to remonstrate against abuses of our sex and our kind"[11]. Similarly, Sarah Grimke too abandoned limitations for women and protested by saying that, "men and women were created equal… Whatever is right for a man to do, is right for woman… I seek no favors for my sex. I surrender not our claim to equality. All is ask of our brethren is, that they will take their feet from off our necks and permit us to stand upright on that ground which God destined us to occupy"[12].

Harriet Taylor Mill (1807 – 1858) and **John Stuart Mill** (1806 – 1873) were two main figures who incorporated and expanded liberal feminist ideas of Mary Wollstonecraft in the latter half of the 19th century. They wrote two essays, 'The Enfranchisement of Women' (1851) and 'On the Subjection of Women' (1869) to illustrate their inclination to fight against sexual discrimination. Harriet Taylor said, "Like Wollstonecraft, I acknowledge that the domestic chores which women are expected to fulfill on a daily basis occupy most of their time and energy"[5]. J.S. Mill's essay argued against essentialism and remarked, "It is ridiculous that any person or doctrine can purport to "know" the nature of the two sexes"[5]. Mill introduced an amendment to the 1867 Reform Act by substituting the word 'person' for the word 'man', after he became an MP.

Caroline Norton (Born March 22, 1808- June 15, 1877) left her mark in the literary forum of the Victorian era. Caroline Elizabeth Sarah Norton was British writer and also a social reformer. She is remembered for her major contribution to secure legal rights for married women in case of matrimonial difficulties.

She got married to the honourable George Norton but this matrimonial knot did not turn out to be fortunate for her. She was denied access to her children, which eventually led her to fight and bring in the Infant custody bill. She also suffered in various other emotional and financial ways by her husband who did not give her any allowance and also demanded money from her. Denied access to see her children instilled a force in her to fight against the law. She used her literary skills and persuaded her campaign via letters and political Pamphlets. She wanted to bring awareness among the public towards the plight of mothers. 'Observations on the Natural Claim of the Mother to the Custody of Her Infant Children as Affected by the Common Law Right of the Father' was her first published pamphlet in 1837. Her second pamphlet was titled, 'The Separation of Mother and the Child by the Law of Custody of Infants considered'. She argued that children below the age of 7 years must live with their mothers, and for older children's custody it should be the court which should decide who shall get the custody, not the father.

Lucretia Mott (January 3rd 1793 - November 11th 1880) was a social reformer, abolitionist, a U.S. Quaker, and a women's rights activist. She possessed excellent speaking skills that helped her becoming an abolitionist and a feminist. She worked for the right to vote for the people who were slaves earlier. She had a major contribution when the Declaration of Sentiments was written during the 1848 Seneca Falls convention. She had given her views on how a harmonious marriage should be. She believed that, "in the marriage union, the independence of the husband and wife will be equal, their dependence mutual, and their obligations reciprocal."[13]

Elizabeth Cady Stanton (November 12, 1815 - October 26, 1902) was a social activist lecturer author, chief founder of the women's rights movement, abolitionist and an American suffragist. Elizabeth Cady felt discontented for women housewife inside the four domestic walls. She motivated herself to take active measures as a remedy to improvise the society in general and women in particular. After knowing the legal status of women and the oppression they had been going through, intensified her thoughts and forced her to step towards arrangement of protest and arguments via public meetings.

Emmeline Pankhurst (15 July 1858 – 14 June 1928) had a major contribution in fighting for the right to vote for women. She became the feminist leader of the women's social and political Union (WSPU). She had two sons and three daughters who accompanied her in the suffrage campaign. The eldest daughter Christabel wrote her mother's biography, which was published posthumously in 1959. The biography was named as 'Unshackled: The story of how we won the vote'. First biography was written by another daughter of hers Sylvia Pankhurst, which is considered as full-length biography of Emmeline Pankhurst. It was called as 'The life of Emmeline Pankhurst' and was published in 1935.

The Second Wave

An anthropologist, Lionel Tiger, in his book 'The Decline of the Male', recognizes the introduction of contraceptive pills as the trigger to the second wave of feminism. Many feminist thinkers believe that the pill gave women power over men.

Simone de Beauvoir is best understood as a bridge between the two waves, as she appeared in the interim. Her frank and notorious explanation of women's oppression in her book 'The Second Sex' (1949) propelled feminist thinkers. Her revolutionary ideas appeared at a time when abortion and contraceptives were illegal and not accessible in most of the countries. Beauvoir argued that the hierarchical division of men and women is not natural, rather framed. Her work was strongly influenced by 'existentialism', which rejects the existence of pre-determined human nature. She argued, that a woman is always situated as 'other' and not as 'I'. This idea was precipitated by the theories of Sigmund Freud, who centralized in his theory of sexuality by the possession of phallus/penis. Thus, according to Freud, women were incomplete since they lack the phallus. Beauvoir asserted that biological differences do not fetch an acceptable explanation to women's oppression, however, the reproductive function has been a disadvantage which binds them to the domestic sphere.

'Gynocritics', is a term coined by an American theorist, **Elaine Showalter** to outline literary criticism based in a feminine perspective. 'Toward a Feminine Poetics' and 'Feminist Criticism in the Wilderness' are two of her essays that have been greatly appreciated. Showalter has divided the history of women's literature into three phases:

i. Feminine (1840-1880)

ii. Feminist (1880-1920)

iii. Female (1920- present)

Betty Friedan is universally considered an important figure of the second wave of feminism. Her book 'The Feminine Mystique' (1963) questioned the assumption of society that women feel totally contended with household chores. Absolute domestic adherence and societal idealistic pressures on women did not leave any space for inclination towards career, financial independence or even higher education. It brought attention to the so-far un-named issue which led American women to a sense of disappointment. Betty begins the book with the first chapter titled as 'The Problem that Has No Name'. Later in the second chapter she describes how a woman's life is completely devoted to the 3ks as per a German slogan: "Kinder, Kuche, Kirche"[14] which means children, kitchen, church. Housewives busy in handling every small event of the family and in upbringing their children are simply unaware of the vacuum developing inside them. Their preoccupied conscious state masks their dreams and ideas. As Friedan points out after reading a women's magazine, that, "it would seem that the concrete details of women's lives are more interesting than their thoughts, their ideas, their dreams."[14]

Another immensely influential work which fought against patriarchy in twentieth century America is **Kate Millett's** 'Sexual

Politics', published in 1970. It added more momentum to the already existing pool of literature supporting second wave of feminism. She argued that male-supremacy is the foundation of all other unequal social structure oppressing women. She denounces "It is interesting that many women do not recognize themselves as discriminated against; no better proof could be found of the totality of their conditioning."[15]

Male dominance seemed to bear an infinite structure since our system has always been based on sexual selection. **Naomi Wolf** (b. 1962) in her book 'The Beauty Myth' says, "Beauty is a currency system like the gold standard. Like any economy, it is determined by politics, and in modern age in the West it is the last, best belief system that keeps male dominance intact."[16] Societal set-up has restricted beauty standards to physical appearance only. Naomi Wolf suggests that, "If we are to free ourselves from the dead weight that has once again been made out of femaleness, it is not ballots or lobbyists or placards that women will need first; it is a new way to see."[16]

The Third Wave

After 1990s, Feminism branched out into several divergent groups such as Amazon Feminism, Analytical Feminism, Anarchist Feminism, Atheist Feminism, Black Feminism, Eco Feminism, Islamic Feminism, Lesbian Feminism, Marxist Feminism, Post-colonial Feminism, etc.

Every debate of feminism has a central and unified theme running through it, which is essentialism. Essentialism is a doctrine which places essence prior to existence. With respect to feminist theories, it reflects that both genders of humans, male and female, have intrinsically unique and different characteristics or dispositions. The point of argument has been broadly based upon ideas that women and men are not just different biologically but also because they behave differently. Essentialists had believed in non-identical attributes of men and women. As per their conjecture, women are endowed with qualities which make them more co-operative and compassionate, more interconnected and harmonious to others. Men, on the contrary, are believed to be authoritarian, rigid, rational, and judicious. Simone de Beauvoir, who had a marked influence on feminist theory and feminist existentialism, did not believe in sexual differences. She argued that these differences are an outcome of cultural conditioning. Her historical account 'The second Sex' elaborates on women's handicapped position in society. She implements three theories in order to explain the condition of women. Her focus remains on biology, psychoanalysis and historical materialism, since none of these could account every aspect of women's situation independently. She holds history as an important factor in contributing to today's condition. Treatment of women by primitive societies has marked them inferior to men as per de Beauvoir. Institutionalized oppression of women as mere private assets by men is deeply acknowledged by her. Her standpoint also depicts religion as another method to subjugate women in the name of moral values. Other excuses, which were inhibiting women's growth, were reproduction, labour, and sexuality.

Women, regarded as 'Other' in her primary research which denotes well-articulated suppression of women in different roles and different ways. 'An Oxford Guide' on Literary Theory & Criticism states about 'The Second Sex' that, "De Beauvoir constructed an epic account of gender division throughout history, examining biological, psychological, historical and cultural explanations for the reduction of women to a second and lesser sex."[17]

Her ideology was heavily influenced by existentialism. She too denied to the existence of an innate nature of men and women which could govern their freedom and responsibilities. Her standpoint stated that a woman is always placed as the 'other' to a man. The man always stood as 'self' or as 'I', which woman was the object situated as 'other' in the periphery of male existence. It would not be incorrect to understand her stance in a way which positions man as the 'subject' and woman as an 'object'. Sigmund Freud's theory of psychoanalysis resonates with her school of thoughts. Freudian analysis based the theory of sexuality on the possession of penis/phallus. Since phallus is present in man, woman is graded a position which is negative or lacking. This phallocentric vision can be detected in various art and literature works too, where woman appeared as a mere object to man's desires. A woman's body played a dominant role in her state of identity, while in case of man; it was mind which was active and supreme. In words of Simone de Beauvoir,

"Woman? Very simple, say those who like simple answers: she is a womb, an ovary; she is a female: this word is enough to define her."[1]

FEMINISM IN INDIAN CONTEXT

Feminism in India seems to have various backgrounds based on different social and religious traditions. India marked the presence of the flame of feminism in the post-independence era. Surprisingly, men started feminist writings in India. Rabindranath Tagore's bold female characters in his novels 'Choker Bali' and 'Ghare Bhaire' prove the same. Kamala Das is the first feminist writer to write in English. Chitra Divakar is another name known for her strong feminist ideologies. She wrote Mahabharata in her book Palace of Illusions from the perspective of Draupadi. Many more women writers came into light that broke the shackles of society and showed best of their skills freely.

Characteristics that defined a true woman have been submissiveness, domesticity, purity and piety. Role of women were confined only to four walls of a house and her sole responsibility was to look after her family and give birth to children to enhance family tree. Women's role and position always comes secondary to her male counterparts. Her say is not counted in any important decisions of the family. Women's subjugation has been there in various ways, be it via practicing polygamy, sati pratha, isolation during widowhood, child marriage, deprivation from education, domesticity, physical abuse, financial dependence etc. such anti-women stereotypes are deep-rooted and dominant in Indian society. These were probably seated in Indian minds from the Indian mythologies and historical traditions. It is quite obvious to say so, since it was not only men but also women were biased towards themselves. Rich mesh works of culture and myths have been ruling minds to an extent where a woman fails to realize her own rights and roles. It is quite typical and accustomed to accept the image of a woman who is a delicate and feeble being, who is in extreme distress and who is defenseless.

Indian women psyche was always shadowed by the image of Sita, who sets paramount example of sacrifice, dedication, virtuosity and devotion to her husband Lord Rama in the epic Ramayana. Sita has been set as an ideal for every girl to follow in her own lifespan so as to achieve highest standard of womanly virtues. The most discussed act from the Ramayana which has been influencing and invoking our minds is Sita's Agnipariksha. Although Sita has set an example of courage too, when she choses the subtle way and denies to further humiliation by requesting to mother Earth to accept her back for all time. Sita was graceful and sober, while Draupadi from another epic Mahabharata was full of aggression and power. The historical instance, which eventually led to the great Mahabharata war, was the game of dice. Her husband Yudhisthira puts Draupadi, also known as Krishna, at stake after he loses everything. Even after several attempts to save herself from the humiliation, Draupadi was stripped and was called a prostitute in an assembly of highly ranked men and family. Even the fiery Draupadi could not save herself from that excruciating insult. It is an evident sign of a biased history which approved of a woman's humiliation. When a queen like Draupadi could not rescue herself from such traumatizing circumstances, and was treated like an object, it is quite apparent and understandable that what the situation must be like for common women then.

Such feminist characters have marked hallmarks of Indian mythology. An ancient verse assembles together the most astonished and remembered fiery female figures from Indian epics in the given way:

> "Ahalya Draupadi Kunti Tara Mandodri tatha
> Panchakanya smaranittyam mahapataka nashaka"[18]

Influence of these women has been utterly dominant on Indian women psyche for centuries. These women demonstrated epitomes of chastity, sacrifice, purity and loyalty. It is important to identify distinction between 'self' and 'identity, so as to justify not even self-image but also relationships and personal arenas like marriage, family life and education.

CONCLUSION

Ideologies of prominent feminist writers like Mary Wollstonecraft, Virginia Woolf, Abigail Adams, Grimke sisters (Sarah Grimke and Angelina Grimke), Harriet Taylor Mill, John Stuart Mill, Simone De Beauvoir, Elaine Showalter, Betty Friedan, Kate Millet, Naomi Wolf etc. have been included to form a background of the wave of feminism. These writers' role is indispensable in the onset of feminism. They struggled and made place for women writers and made their work appreciable without any prejudice. Some of their works like 'A Vindication of the Rights of Woman', 'A Room of one's own', 'The Second Sex' and 'Toward a Feminine Poetics' are a few milestones of this discourse. The history of feminism is incomplete without these names.

Myths created time and again have been the seeds which grew to a system called patriarchy. A major factor, which denounces the order of genders, is that, that women species have been seen as secondary. Woman's existence, just like her male counterparts', must not encompass either of body, mind and soul, but all. It is essential to understand the value of 'identity' and 'self' in relation to each other. Women must rise above the feeling of their bodies only, and should realize the needed importance of their existence as a moral being too. As Jasbir Jain puts it;

> "Freedom of the body would allow the intellect to gain supremacy."[19]

References

1. de Beauvoir, Simone. *The Second Sex.* London, Vintage Books, 2011.

2. Mccartney, Kathleen. "Happy 80th Gloria Steinem" Web. 15 Mar 2014. <https://edition.cnn.com/2014/03/24/opinion/mcccartney-steinem-at-80/index.html>.

3. Moran, Caitlin. *How To Be a Woman.* New York: Ebury Random House Group, 2011. 88.

4. Anderson, G.D. Web. 23 Sep. 2015. <https://gdanderson.com/>.

5. Jenainati, Cathia, and Judy Groves. *Introducing Feminism: A Graphic Guide.* London: Icon, 2010. 5.

6. Allen, Prudence. *The Concept of Woman.* Grand Rapids, MI: William. B. Eerdmans, 1997. 98.

7. Wollstonecraft, Mary, and Cadace Ward. "The Prevailing Opinion of a Sexual Character Discussed" *A Vindication of the Rights of Woman.* Mineola, NY: Dover Publications, 1996.

8. Woolf, Virginia, *A Room of One's Own.* London, Penguin Classics, 2000.

9. Barker-Benfield, G.J. *Abigail and John Adams: The Americanization of Sensibility.* Chicago: University of Chicago, 2010. 193.

10. Gelles, Edith Belle. *Portia: The World of Abigail Adams.* Bloomington: Indiana UP, 1992. 48.

11. Neuman, Johanna. *And Yet They Persisted: How American Women Won the Right to Vote.* Hoboken, NJ: Wiley-Blackwell,2019. 36.

12. Dillner, Luisa. *The Complete Book of Sisters.* London: Faber& Faber, 2010.

13. Mott, Lucretia. *Discourse on Woman.* Philadelphia, USA:T. B. Peterson, 1850.

14. Friedan, Betty. *The Feminine Mystique.* London: Penguin Modern Classics, 2010. 39.

15. <http://www.nytimes.com/2017/09/06/obituaries/kate-millett-influential-feminist-writer-is-dead-at-82.html>.

16. Wolf, Naomi. *The Beauty Myth.* London: Vintage Books, 1991. 19.

17. Waugh, Patricia. *Literary Theory and Criticism.* New Delhi: Oxford UP, 2011.

18. Bhattacharya, Pradip. "Living by Their Own Norms: Unique Powers of the *Panchkanyas*." *Manushi*. 145. 30-37. Web. 27 Sep. 2015. <http://www.manushi-india.org/pdfs_issues/PDF%20145/Panchkayana%2030-37.pdf>.

19. Jain, Jasbir. *Indigenous Roots of Feminism: Culture, Subjectivity and Agency*. New Delhi: SAGE, 2011. 4.

11

Women Empowerment in India

-CHR Raina Khatri Tandon

Founder Right2Rise & RKT Foundation
(Posh Pocso Specialist & Limitless
*Enabler ,Human rights Social Activist ,Thought Leader
President of WICCI T&D MAHARASTRA ,ALL ,
Women Economic Forum (2017-2020)*

"You can tell the condition of a nation by looking at the status of its women" **– Pt. Jawaharlal Nehru**

Why we talk about women empowerment only and not men empowerment? Why women need empowerment and not men? Women make almost 70% of the total population of the world. Then why this substantial section of the society needs empowerment? They are not in minority so as to require special treatment. Biologically speaking also, it is a proven fact that female race is superior to male. Then the question arises that why we are debating the topic 'Women Empowerment'. ARE THEY NOT EMPOWERED ?

"You wanna fly, you got to give up the shit that weighs you down."

Why we Need women Empowerment?

"A girl should be two things: who and what she wants." – Coco Chanel

Need for empowerment arose due to centuries of domination and discrimination done by men over women; women are the suppressed lot. They are the target of varied types of violence and discriminatory practices done by men all over the world. India is no different.

India is a complex country.It's a democratic republican yet it completely doesn't follow giving the essential UN CHARTERED rights and follow them in our systems completely and wholly. We have, through centuries, developed various types of customs, traditions and practices. These customs and traditions, good as well as bad, have become a part of our society's collective consciousness. We worship female goddesses; we also give great importance to our mothers, daughters, sisters, wives and other female relatives or friends. But at the same time, Indians are also famous for treating their women badly both inside and outside their homes.

Indian society consists of people belonging to almost all kinds of religious beliefs. In every religion women are given a special place and every religion teaches us to treat women with respect and dignity. But somehow the society has so developed that various types of ill practices, both physical and mental, against women have become a norm since ages. For instance, sati pratha, practice of dowry, parda pratha, female infanticide, wife burning, sexual violence, sexual harassment at work place, domestic violence and other varied kinds of discriminatory practices; all such acts consists of physical as well as mental element.

The reasons for such behaviour against women are many but the most important one are the male superiority complex and patriarchal system of society. Though to eliminate these ill practices and discrimination against women various constitutional and legal rights are there but in reality there are a lot to be done. Several self-help groups and NGOs are working in this direction; also women themselves are breaking the societal barriers and achieving great heights in all dimensions: political, social and economic. But society as a whole has still not accepted women as being equal to men and crimes or abuses against women are still on the rise. For that to change, the society's age-old deep-rooted mind set needs to be changed through social conditioning and sensitization programmes.

Therefore, the concept of women empowerment not only focuses on giving women strength and skills to rise above from their miserable situation but at the same time it also stresses on the need to educate men regarding women issues and inculcating a sense of respect and duty towards women as equals. In the present write-up we will try to describe and understand the concept of Women Empowerment in India in all its dimensions.

What is Women Empowerment

Women empowerment in simple words can be understood as giving power to women to decide for their own lives or inculcating such abilities in them so that they could be able to find their rightful place in the society.

According to the **United Nations**, women's empowerment mainly has five components:

- Generating women's sense of self-worth;
- Women's right to have and to determine their choices;
- Women's right to have access to equal opportunities and all kinds of resources;
- Women's right to have the power to regulate and control their own lives, within and outside the home; and
- Women's ability to contribute in creating a more just social and economic order.

Thus, women empowerment is nothing but recognition of women's basic human rights and creating an environment where they are treated as equals to men.

Women Empowerment in India

Historical Background:

From ancient to modern period, women's condition-socially, politically and economically- has not remained same and it kept changing with times. In ancient India, women were having equal status with men; in early Vedic period they were very educated and there are references of women sages such as Maitrayi in our ancient texts. But with the coming of famous treatise of Manu i.e. Manusmriti, the status of women was relegated to a subordinate position to men.

"I myself have never been able to find out precisely what feminism is: I only know that people call me a feminist whenever I express sentiments that differentiate me from a doormat, or a prostitute."

All kinds of discriminatory practices started to take from such as child marriage, devadashi pratha, nagar vadhu system, sati pratha etc. Women's socio-political rights were curtailed and they were made fully dependent upon the male members of family. Their right to education, right to work and right to decide for themselves were taken away.

During medieval period the condition of women got worsened with the advent of Muslim rulers in India; as also during the British period. But the British rule also brought western ideas into the country.

"As long as she thinks of a man, nobody objects to a woman thinking." – Virginia Woolf, Orlando

A few enlightened Indians such as Raja Ram Mohan Roy influenced by the modern concept of freedom, liberty, equality and justice started to question the prevailing discriminatory practices against women. Through his unrelenting efforts, the British were forced to abolish the ill-practice of Sati. Similarly, several other social reformers such as Ishwar Chandra Vidyasagar, Swami Vivekananda, Acharya Vinoba Bhave etc. worked for the upliftment of women in India. For instance, the Widow Remarriage Act of 1856 was the result of Ishwar Chandra Vidyasagar's movement for improving the conditions of widows.

"Incredible change happens in your life when you decide to take control of what you do have power over instead of craving control over what you don't."

Indian National Congress supported the first women's delegation which met the Secretary of State to demand women's political rights in 1917. The Child Marriage Restraint Act in 1929 was passed due to the efforts of Mohammad Ali Jinna, Mahatma Gandhi called upon the young men to marry the child widows and urged people to boycott child marriages.

During freedom movement, almost all the leaders of the struggle were of the view that women should be given equal status in the free India and all types of discriminatory practices must stop. And for that to happen, it was thought fit to include such provisions in the Constitution of India which would help eliminate age-old exploitative customs and traditions and also such provisions which would help in empowering women socially, economically and politically.

Constitution of India and Women Empowerment

India's Constitution makers and our founding fathers were very determined to provide equal rights to both women and men. The Constitution of India is one of the finest equality documents in the world. It provides provisions to secure equality in general and gender equality in particular. Various articles in the Constitution safeguard women's rights by putting them at par with men socially, politically and economically.

The Preamble, the Fundamental Rights and other constitutional provisions provide several general and special safeguards to secure women's human rights.

Preamble

The Preamble to the Constitution of India assures justice, social, economic and political; equality of status and opportunity and dignity to the individual. Thus , it treats both men and women equal.

Fundamental Rights

The policy of women empowerment is well entrenched in the Fundamental Rights enshrined in our Constitution. For instance:

- Article 14 ensures to women the right to equality.

- Article 15(1) specifically prohibits discrimination on the basis of sex.
- Article 15(3) empowers the State to take affirmative actions in favour of women.
- Article 16 provides for equality of opportunity for all citizens in matters relating to employment or appointment to any office.

These rights being fundamental rights are justiciable in court and the Government is obliged to follow the same.

Directive Principles of State Policy:

Directive principles of State Policy also contains important provisions regarding women empowerment and it is the duty of the government to apply these principles while making laws or formulating any policy. Though these are not justiciable in the Court but these are essential for governance nonetheless. Some of them are:

- Article 39 (a) provides that the State to direct its policy towards securing for men and women equally the right to an adequate means of livelihood.
- Article 39 (d) mandates equal pay for equal work for both men and women.
- Article 42 provides that the State to make provision for securing just and humane conditions of work and for maternity relief.

Fundamental Duties:

Fundamental duties are enshrined in Part IV-A of the Constitution and are positive duties for the people of India to follow. It also contains a duty related to women's rights:

Article 51 (A) (e) expects from the citizen of the country to promote harmony and the spirit of common brotherhood amongst all the people of India and to renounce practices derogatory to the dignity of women.

Other Constitutional Provisions:

Through 73rd and 74th Constitutional Amendment of 1993, a very important political right has been given to women which is a landmark in the direction of women empowerment in India. With this amendment women were given 33.33 percent reservation in seats at different levels of elections in local governance i.e., at Panchayat, Block and Municipality elections.

Thus, it can be seen that these Constitutional provisions are very empowering for women and the State is duty bound to apply these principles in taking policy decisions as well as in enacting laws.

Specific Laws for Women Empowerment in India

Here is the list of some specific laws which were enacted by the Parliament in order to fulfil Constitutional obligation of women empowerment:

- The Equal Remuneration Act, 1976.
- The Dowry Prohibition Act, 1961.
- The Immoral Traffic (Prevention) Act, 1956.
- The Maternity Benefit Act, 1961.
- The Medical termination of Pregnancy Act, 1971.
- The Commission of Sati (Prevention) Act, 1987.
- The Prohibition of Child Marriage Act, 2006.
- The Pre-Conception & Pre-Natal Diagnostic Techniques (Regulation and Prevention of Misuse) Act, 1994.
- The Sexual Harassment of Women at Work Place (Prevention, Protection and) Act, 2013.

Above mentioned and several other laws are there which not only provide specific legal rights to women but also gives them a sense of security and empowerment.

International Commitments of India as to Women Empowerment

India is a part to various International conventions and treaties which are committed to secure equal rights of women.

One of the most important among them is the Convention on Elimination of All Forms of Discrimination against Women (CEDAW), ratified by India in 1993.

Other important International instruments for women empowerment are: The Mexico Plan of Action (1975), the Nairobi Forward Looking Strategies (1985), the Beijing Declaration as well as the Platform for Action (1995) and the Outcome Document adopted by the UNGA Session on Gender Equality and Development & Peace for the 21st century, titled "Further actions and initiatives to implement the Beijing Declaration and the Platform for Action". All these have been whole-heartedly endorsed by India for appropriate follow up.

These various national and International commitments, laws and policies notwithstanding women's situation on the ground have still not improved satisfactorily. Varied problems related to women are still subsisting; female infanticide is growing, dowry is still prevalent, domestic violence against women is practised; sexual harassment at workplace and other heinous sex crimes against women are on the rise.

Though, economic and social condition of women has improved in a significant way but the change is especially visible only in metro cities or in urban areas; the situation is not much improved in semi-urban areas and villages. This disparity is due to lack of education and job opportunities and negative mind set of the society which does not approve girls' education even in 21st century.

Government Policies and Schemes for Women Empowerment

Whatever improvement and empowerment women have received is especially due to their own efforts and struggle, though governmental schemes are also there to help them in their endeavour.

In the year 2001, the Government of India launched a **National Policy for Empowerment of Women**. The specific objectives of the policy are as follows:

- Creation of an environment through positive economic and social policies for full development of women to enable them to realize their full potential.
- Creation of an environment for enjoyments of all human rights and fundamental freedom by women on equal basis with men in all political, economic, social, cultural and civil spheres.
- Providing equal access to participation and decision making of women in social political and economic life of the nation.
- Providing equal access to women to health care, quality education at all levels, career and vocational guidance, employment, equal remuneration, occupational health and safety, social security and public life etc.
- Strengthening legal systems aimed at elimination of all forms of discrimination against women.
- Changing societal attitudes and community practices by active participation and involvement of both men and women.
- Mainstreaming a gender perspective in the development process.
- Elimination of discrimination and all forms of violence against women and the girl child.
- Building and strengthening partnerships with civil society, particularly women's organizations.

The Ministry of Women and Child Development is the nodal agency for all matters pertaining to welfare, development and empowerment of women. It has evolved schemes and programmes for their benefit. These schemes are spread across a very wide spectrum such as women's need for shelter, security, safety, legal aid, justice, information, maternal health, food, nutrition etc., as well as their need for economic sustenance through skill development, education and access to credit and marketing.

Various schemes of the Ministry are like Swashakti, Swayamsidha, STEP and Swawlamban enable economic empowerment. Working Women Hostels and Creches provide support services. Swadhar and Short Stay Homes provide protection and rehabilitation to women in difficult circumstances. The Ministry also supports autonomous bodies like National Commission, Central Social Welfare Board and Rashtriya Mahila Kosh which work for the welfare and development of women. Economic sustenance of women through skill development, education and access to credit and marketing is also one of the areas where the Ministry has special focus.

"She is free in her wildness, she is a wanderess, a drop of free water. She knows nothing of borders and cares nothing for rules or customs. 'Time' for her isn't something to fight against. Her life flows clean, with passion, like fresh water.

Conclusion and Suggestions:

In conclusion, it can be said that women in India, through their own unrelenting efforts and with the help of Constitutional and other legal provisions and also with the aid of Government's various welfare schemes, are trying to find their own place under the sun. And it is a heartening sign that their participation in employment- government as well as private, in socio-political activities of the nation and also their presence at the highest decision-making bodies is improving day by day.

"Women are always saying, 'We can do anything that men can do.' But Men should be saying, We can do anything that women can do."

However, we are still far behind in achieving the equality and justice which the Preamble of our Constitution talks about. The real problem lies in the patriarchal and male-dominated system of our society which considers women as subordinate to men and creates different types of methods to subjugate them.

The need of us is to educate and sensitize male members of the society regarding women issues and try to inculcate a feeling of togetherness and equality among them so that they would stop their discriminatory practices towards the fairer sex.

"If you look at what you have in life,
You'll always have more.
If you look at what you don't have in life,
You'll never have enough."

For this to happen apart from Government, the efforts are needed from various NGOs and from enlightened citizens of the country. And first of all, efforts should begin from our homes where we must empower female members of our family by providing them equal opportunities of education, health, nutrition and decision making without any discrimination.

Because India can become a powerful nation only if it truly empowers its women.

"A woman is the full circle. Within her is the power to create, nurture and transform." :GO GET IT !

12

Gender Equality in Classical Antiquity

Souhardya De

FRAS and Columnist

The Indic and the Graeco-Roman civilisations, often considered to be the powerhouses of the ancient world, have always demented scholars, (when seen through the various periods of their upbringing) about the ideologies and the status, women had to play in societal developments.

Taking into consideration the various epics and literary sources that form a major part of the ancient Indian scriptures, gender equality seems not to be a thing scholars be bothered about. Seemingly because, the Indus Civilisation (or what we might also denominate as the Harappan civilisation and what came before the Aryan race established its hegemony) had always had an all powerful deity who was indeed feminine, as has been observed by classicists and archaeologists who have unearthed the figurine statuettes of the Mother Goddesses at various locations throughout the territory of the Indus civilisation .

For a society or a civilisation that worships women, gender inequality seems to have been a thing not extant. Talking of the then contemporary cases such as the Minoan Civilisation at Crete, it could be well noted that the frescoes have often depicted women, beautifully robed, symbolic of the freedom to enforce their wills. Thus, there arises no question of inequality in these times, if seen through the blurred out lenses of a classical demeanour.

But, when deepened into the intricate observations, assumptions and eventually, conclusions would alter. In fact, the frescoes and goddesses talked about until now, are but, women who belonged to the upper classes of the society.

Societal hierarchy is a thing that was prevalent from the days when human learnt to group himself into clusters. Not surprisingly, the members of the royal family could, as of now, enjoy their own rights and had no bindings that could affix them. In fact, the Greek myths widely deal with stories of heroes and their spouses who are again, in an attempt to emphasise upon their aristocratic belonging, often depicted as heroines. What was the social status of the slaves who were bought and sold? Did their females enjoy the power to choose their own partners or were they just set aside from this custom and were destined to be concubines forever? The questions remain unanswered.

Greek mythology has, in its various legendary tales about their pantheon, depicted the male gods as fearless, vile, ferocious and war loving; characteristics that, in their opinions, suit that of a man, while females like Hera and Demeter are generally not associated with weapons. In fact, most of the Greek goddesses (other than Athena and Artemis who have equal capabilities to that of Ares and Apollo) have always been associated with harvesting, crop ripening, beauty and love. Such were formed the listed characteristic traits associated with or attributed to the feminine gender: gentle, tender, loving and caring.

Mythology gave rise to gender inequality and questions have been risen on whether a woman is sufficient enough to take care of herself or whether she has to depend on her male partner for her life and her safety.

In the Indian classical text, Ramayana, although Sita is eventually identified as an avatar of Lakshmi, the goddess of wealth, she's shown to be helpless at Ashoka Vatika, under Ravana's captivity, if it were really her (scholars have, in the past few decades, disagreed over the actual identity of the woman kept confined at Ravana's garden in Lanka). But when talking about the original storyline of the epic, it was Lord Ram who rescued her, after a vociferous battle that crushed the authority of the Asuras and extended the banner of the Raghukula till the Deccan or to the Dravidians (only if Rama can be considered to be a proper Aryan).

Classicist Don Nardo, in his book entitled 'Women of Ancient Greece' has closely observed the political, social and economic conditions of the women who lived back then. A brief interpretation of his analysis would lead us to observe that even though women could not participate in political discussions or orations at the senate, they could still enjoy a certain degree of freedom, until the Archaic age. Thus there arises no doubts on the fact that women weren't equal to men.

Although, in his thesis entitled, "Debating Women's Equality: Toward a Feminist Theory of Law from a European Perspective" Ute Gerard says that women often owned land, as found from the records of ancient Delphi, Gortyn, Thessaly, Megara and Sparta, Athenian women were simply regarded to be a part of the 'oikos' (En: household) that was usually dominated by a male family head or a kyrios (En: master). The spouse was often referred to as the 'damar', which, in English terms, transliterates to 'to tame'. Thus, the condition of the Athenian women, when seen through the perspectives of them being a part of the household, were no different to the conditions of the Indian women who were dominated by their male family members; a system that came to be called as patriarchy.

Comparing closely, Indian women had a better position in the society during the Early Vedic Period, when she could attend festival rites, yagnas, choose her own husband through the means of swayamvara and often, participate in philosophical discussions with leading sages (instances include Maitreyi and Gargi).

As the society evolved and the class and caste structures became complicated, the female was stripped off all her societal dignity and all relaxations given to her earlier, were snatched away. The brahmanical superiority began to find its way, around this period. Nevertheless, swayamvara remained but only in name.

Talking again about the Indian classics, Ramayana and the Mahabharata, we have seen both caste discriminations and the prevalence of a not so idealistic swayamvara. Both Rama and Arjuna had to fulfil the tasks set for them to wed Sita and Draupadi respectively. It might have been that Rama was an able human and of course, since he was the avatar of the Lord on earth, caring and affectionate for his better half. But that didn't mean that Sita was free to choose Rama. They could only unite when Rama could string the bow, hence fulfilling the requirements set for a prince to have Sita's hand in marriage.

In the Mahabharata, when all princes could attempt in piercing the eye of a fish kept on a revolving disk, by looking at its reflection in the water below (the condition set for the Swayamvara), Karna, a very efficient archer and originally, son of Kunti, was set aside only because people thought that he was a Sutaputra (in English terms, a charioteer's son) and was not eligible to participate in a contest that deserved only the royal men.

Such instances have been found in almost all tales of the world. If talking about the Greek mythology, when Troy was won over by Hercules, the Greek God of Strength and Masculinity, Hesione, princess of Troy and daughter of King Laomedon, was given away to Hercules' partner Telamon, one who had helped him in breaching the Trojan walls, ultimately to be made into his concubine.

Coming back to the Athenian discussion, women were exploited like nowhere throughout Greece. They were not even considered true citizens, which is why they had limited property rights and complex divorce processes.

Divorces in Athens were interesting, especially because of the procedure in which they were conducted.

There were three types of divorces, as noted down by Sue Blundell in 'Women in Ancient Greece':

1. By mutual consent of both the partners (the damar and the kyrios)

2. The kyrios or the male household master, when he willed to divorce, could simply throw out the female counterpart from his residence.

3. When the damar had to demand for divorce, she wouldn't be permitted to do so herself. It was because she wasn't even recognised as an Athenian citizen. All she could do was to take the help of her male family members (that included a father, a brother or somebody else) to demand for a divorce, as per the legal terms.

Thus, in simpler words, a woman was always considered the property of a man. The earlier stages of her life were to be dominated by her father's decisions, be that effectual or ineffectual, whereas the later part of her life (after marriage; child marriages were prevalent both in India and Greece) was to be dominated by the kyrios or the master of the household!

When it comes to education though, differences arise between the civilisations. Greek women, in their early childhood, were allowed to attend teachings of a litterator and later, that of a grammaticus, both of which were equivalent to tutors who taught boys!

The only exception arose when the household that the woman came from would be poor. Here, she was expected to stay back at her home, supporting her family in cleaning up the household and working as a maid. But then, the conditions imposed upon the boy were also similar. He wasn't expected to attend school but rather, work in the fields to help sustain his family.

Women have often also been described on detailings of ancient Greek pottery which however, sexualised their depictions to a large extent. In the opinions of Sue Blundell, "Scenes of adornment within vase painting are a window into the women's sphere, though they were not entirely realistic, rather, a product of the voyeuristic and romanticized image of womanhood rooted in the male gaze".

Hence, however advanced (technically, philosophically and literally) and impenetrable these ancient civilisations were, gender equality was never a thing that existed in the classical age, be that Archaic, Hellenic or the Aryan epochs. Gender equality, today, must become a lived reality. The oppression and unjust practices that women had to endure for centuries, had made them bold enough to suppress the oppressors and claim their rights, as they did in Greece, Africa and many other parts of the world. But yet, males haven't actually forgotten the classical ideals. They seem not to realise that gender equality isn't only an issue for women, it is an issue for the human community as a whole, to be extant in it. Emma Watson's words would best fit in the box! "It is time we see gender as a spectrum, instead of two sets of opposing ideals".

13

Gender Equity & Female Empowerment policy for Sustainable Development

Titta Kote

Founder & CEO- The Happy Ambassador Concept, Finland
Marketing Manager, Kipuwex Ltd, Hallituskatu

Gender Equity in Development

This issue is very personal for me, as I'm victim of violence based on religious conflicts. That's the reason why The Happy Ambassador concept for children was born. My life mission is to spread cultural awareness to early education, to increase solidarity, respect towards different cultures and religions. As we all are equal. Everybody should be loved just the way they are, with own beliefs and traditions. This way we can create more loving and peaceful world for everyone. I see highly important to defend women rights worldwide, especially in countries where women issues are not enough valued and treated equally. Freedom to be yourself can sound simple, but it's actually one of the hardest thing for females still in today's world.

I live in Finland and I have faced severe religious conflicts, including death treats, threat of child abduction. They have caused a lot of traumas. I suffer time to time traumatic memory attacks. Like before I have turned traumatic experiences to spread happiness, to create happiness. No matter if we face violence in our lives, we should be allowed to live happily, to aim for personal happiness. In the process it's really important to understand the situation, reasons and effects. Finland has rather good situation in gender equality in general. We had woman President, Mrs Tarja Halonen, our Prime Minister is woman, Mrs. Sanna Marin. Women are seen in high positions. Despite of our good gender equality accoring to laws and rights are very good, in reality statistics are not good. Inside the European Union, in Finland women are victims of violence second most often. Government has started preventive program against zero violence towards women. Preventive programs are in use in kindergardens, schools in working societys. We come to the point, where inviduals actions counts. Laws and programs are not protecting women in terrific acts of violence, it's the citizens, it's work colleagues, it's family members.

I have faced also sexual harassment in numerous cases during my working life. It has been either physical or mental. It's highly important to strive for the betterment of women rights and to talk in schools, working societys, universities and to empower women and girls to understand their rights to set limits and boundaries. Shame is so powerfully related to these sudden situations, that numerous cases remain hidden. Victims are too shamed to talk about it, and they can feel guiltyness. Violence in any form should never be accepted. Every individual should be empowered to maintain selfconfidence and power to report wrong behaviour without fear.

I'm grateful as being voiceless girl and woman, life has given me a path to have a voice. And I want to give my voice and my face to all the girls and women who are victims of violence wether it's mental or physical. This girl who was bullied at school because of voice, this woman who was not allowed to talk because of death threats, threat of child abduction is now voice for every girl and every woman who have faced violence in their lives, and who are not able to talk about it.

If we are born with a voice. How we could express ourselves without voice? How we could express our pain, if life is limiting us to be voiceless. How we could feel ourself important in this society if our voice is not heard wether it is spoken or written, if our thoughts would not matter.

In many cultures females are kept quiet, this is leading to inequality, which is creating unbalanced societys, nations. It's very sad to think, that women are not allowed to be themselves, how child could learn the true personality of the mother, how mother could learn the true nature of a dother. There's unlimited power and knowledge in those women worldwide, who are not allowed to express themselves, who are not allowed to be themselves, to have their dreams, to pursue their passion to make their impact for this world.

By empowering women globally, we can see impacts immediately in families, when women are equaly treated there can be peace inside individuals, there can be peace inside families. It can be chain reaction, creating innovations, work places, economical growth. As everyone of us are equal no matter of our origin, no matter of our gender, no matter of our wealth, when we are born and we die, we all are in the same line. What happens between that, it's important. It's important to have voice for the girls, it's important to have voice for the teenager girls, it's important to have voice for the women, that's one of the women rights. To have freedom for education, to have freedom for career, every individual has their own dreams. Every dream is important. What matters, is to be able to make your own choises. This way each of us can achieve personal happiness, when we are able to pursue own dreams and desires in life, to take care of our wellbeing mentally and physically. By respecting each person as individuals, we strive towards better humanity and harmony, which decreases home violence, bullying, crimes even wars in long haul.

In life there should be always room for tolerance as we all make mistakes. In many cultures are still applied honor murders or family rejection due to religious or cultural conflicts. If the dother or wife is not behaving as suitable according to the values and believes of the head of the family. Again we come to freedom and to the fact, that each of us are individuals.

As my son said, during the short life of yours, you've been through so much. Indeed, so far during the short life of mine, I have experienced a lot. I thank life, for it's interesting experiences. Whether they are good or bad, experiences taste of life. I have learned life lessons. I believe, that the courage and lust for life are causes of major sorrows and huge joys. There was a time, when I lost my ability to cry for some years, because I just had to survive and to take care of my son. I did get the ability back, but I'm not able to show tiers spontaneously in situations, which are emotional. I believe it's due to need to stay strong during the hard times and to hide my pain. I could not break down, no matter what as I had to take care of my child the best possible way to be able to create happy childhood and foundation for his life no matter what were the circumstances around.

It's also important to forgive, to lighten our own path, as personal happiness is creating more peace and harmony around us. Violence against women is severe worldwide problem. According to latest report of United Nations, every 3rd woman has experienced violence. And there's so much violence, which remains hidden. Victims of violence should never think it's shame to talk about it.

It's easy to say so, because I have felt the same. Shame. Victims of violence needs a lot of help for balanced and happy life, as everybody has right to be happy without heavy burden of traumatic memories, which can cause severe health issues. Traumatic memory attacks cause internal pain, which also causes physical pain. No matter how many years has gone by from acts of violence. Due to my own experiences, I want to help women and girls around the world towards happy life.

How we could foster our international relationships and to create sustainable development in different sectors. I really think it's about individual's actions. We need to keep the open mind, the open heart. To see the other cultures as richness. It's really important to promote peace, through friendships, through partnerships, through collaborations. I can't highlight enough, as diversity is my heart issue and I want to spread cultural awareness, to spread peace between different nations, between cultures and countries. The cultural awareness is also important to the adults, to the societys, to the whole world for the betterment of our humanity .

How we maintain the peace? With curiosity, when we meet other people from different cultures, we should try to understand where they are coming from. What are their traditions, their ways, their rules. Especially when we visit other countries we should obey the country rules to maintain the peace. I think, when we respect the differences, diversity and when there's equality, solidarity between people. This is the best way ofcourse to maintain the peace. Because equality is the main thing.

We live in a wonderful world. It's full of fascinating cultures, traditions, delicious foods. We need to respect and to let everybody to be as they want to be, to have their own desires, to have their own way, traditions, their religions. It's about the respect and that's how we can maintain peace. Let's be peace builders by raising cultural awareness with conscience and compassion. Social skills are essential for our identity, how w interact with other people, all leading towards sustainable development. Teaching social skills are essential for the betterment of humanity. To be genuine, honest, but also to be equipped with consideration. Parents and teachers to raise world citizens, who are able to live in peace with good communication skills to negotiate, and to nurture relationships. Mission is to impact already to early education and in long term to create more peace and happiness, less bullying, less racism, less conflicts for the betterment of humanity.

"New reality"

Pandemic, covid-19, unexpected external threat. Different situations can effect to our mindset, bring traumatic flashbacks even there's no direct connection. When there was pandemic in my son's school, I got traumatic flashbacks. It was nothing to do with my traumatic experiences, which are example death treats. I understood, I got traumatic flashback as it brought the feeling to be helpless, powerless, uncertain situation and external life threat factor.

I think global pandemic is testing the mental stage of the world, resilience of the human beings. I'm talking now from perspective of a mother and children aspects. As we know pandemic have had wide and serious concequences. How we show our emotions to our children has a big effect. Do we create hope or fear by our own actions, and children are the best to sense it. They are masters for using many senses. In anycase, pandemic has effected to children's minds.

Does it help if we worry excessively, from my point of view, no it doesn't. It makes us mentally sick, then we become also physically ill. No matter if there's even fear of death or bad financial situation, we should maintain the hopes up, to stay optimistic. We need to program our mindset for sustainable development. Fear and unknown future is easier to cope with when we live in the present. We do our best for ourselves and for our family, we help those who are in need. It can mean simple things, to have peaceful and loving athmosphere and food to eat. It's really back to the basics. I think it's upto ourselves and our energy how much we can take the pressure, and are we going forward with big or small steps. Some days we can jump like lion forward some days just to take the minimal steps.

As Happy Ambassador character and concept for children was born due to traumatic experiences, I could refer that time as a pandemic of my life. I think during difficult times, it's highly important to take care of our mental and physical wellbeing as they are connected. No matter what kind of circumstances are around you. We should concentrate to live in the moment, think what you can do now for the betterment of yourself and for your children. Safe and understanding athmosphere is important at home.

As it's said children are mirrows from parents. It's very important for mothers to maintain their calmness, and not over react and transfer panic to the children. As media is in under children's reach, it causes a lot of questions. I can't highlight enough, parents responsibility to maintain calm and loving athmosphere at home, where open disscussion should be number one.

As I know from the experience, the truth is not hurting the child. When children ask questions, we need to reply honestly, no matter if we think, it's not good for the child. When child wants more information from the difficult topic, they will ask, they will enquire. In this way, it's child orientated way. Also as parents we give example to the children by our actions, and we need to keep the hopes up for the better future. We are the ones who can provide stable life at home even during pandemic and after.

How we can do that? By finding our own balance. How we can do that? By using the tools, what we have. By choosing to be happy. By doing the things, what makes you happy. It's not rocket science, it's simple daily actions and to maintain your innerchild.

To find the happiness inside yourself can be fullday job, but when you learn your own tools, it's easy like brushing your theeths, you learn what makes you happy. Exercises, reading, crafts, playing, baking, possibilities at home are endless. At home we also need to learn to think out of the box. Things are back to basics, when we are not able to go to regular hobbies or schools, working places. If you want to do something, use your creativity as it's like a sunlight for human beings.

Example painting. You don't need to have all equipments. You can use your creativity, you can paint with your fingers, with hair coam, just use your imagination. If you want to dance, take a pillow to your hands, put the music on, use your carpet pictures to create your steps and movements. Same out of the box thinking goes with everything. You can maintain your physical and mental health at home,when you learn what works for you, what are your own tools. I'm not able to say what you like, or you can't say what i should do. I need to know it by myself and take the actions. As without our own desires, without our own voice, we are lost. But we need to stay flexible and to adapt the new ways of living.

We need to have motivation, to have positive attitude, to believe in ourselves. When you use these tools, you became warrior of your own. Your mental and physical health is in balance also your selfconfident has risen, and when there's less people to be negative, or critical towards you, you are brave to be yourself. When you achieve this stage, your mind is not affected anymore even by the negative people or criticism. So work with yourself and you will find happiness.

When you have happiness and peace inside of you, you spread this around you. You spread this in your family, your spread this to your friends, to your loved ones, to your working society, everywhere you go. Conscience, the golden skill inside us to guide our daily actions. It's really important during these days, when we have global pandemic going on. That we find the conscience inside of us and we support each other, we help each other for the better future. We can use our conscience to make the betterments in our own home, we can make the betterments in our working society by individuals actions. When we have compassion, when we have love, when we have kindness towards each other we are bringing much more better environment for everybody. We can apply the conscience in our daily life. Yes, I'm also applying conscience in my daily life. I believe with the kindness and when you keep your path on truth, the truth always wins in the end.

Like it said health is our wealth. This is so true. That's the biggest wealth on earth for human beings. Without health, what we can do. I could say mental health is even more important than physical. To believe for the better future. Rule number one, giving up is not an option. And actually now, this time when the world stopped, I hope every individual stopped to think, what is my passion, what I want to do in this life and to pursue those things.

There are also positive impacts of Covid-19. It's effecting people in deeper level. When we are forced to slow down, we have more time to think what is essential in our lives. We think more about our physical and mental wellbeing. We start to use food more like a medicine than a petrol, by healthier choices. We use more our senses, to see, to feel, to hear our innerself and our needs. It's kind of multisensory learning. We learn to be better towards ourselves and others. Humanity is rising, there's more kindness, you can see more smiles from strangers. People are learning to act with one for all, all for one mentality. Nothing is for granted, love your past, love your future. As Covid-19 is a global pandemic, it's also building bridges between different cultures with humanity.

There's always positive aspects in every situation, even in painful situations. We learn, we are life time learners. I have worked from home for years.The respect for the home office people are rising, people who work from home are new normal. That suits me well, I hope you will learn to love it too. Working from home office is not stopping you, instead it's giving limitless opportunities if you are open minded and I recommend it for all the women around the world!

Empowering females, what is it that makes a woman to create, to innovate, to pursue own dreams in work field. What makes women Entrepreneurs to try their upmost? Built-in fire, creativity, the joy, the desire to show, competitive instinct. Entrepreneurship requirements list is endless. I have to be this and that, to learn continuously, to be up to date. To acquire knowledge from various topics, to be master in different sub-regions. Dive into new worlds, especially when economically is tight. When it is impossible to hire workers, buy external expertise. The answer is learning new things, which results in the accumulation of other things. Such a twist shout its existence already very easily. Where one person is enough? We can be super people, super-achievers, but we are not machines. A person also needs other things. We are not machines that are powered indefinitely. Neither even machines can not stand forever. That's why it's important to take care of your own overall wellbeing each and every day.

I talk about women empowerment, but same time you can understand the importance of fathers. How my father has impacted in my life is priceless. We come to gender equality. In order to flourish as individuals in our societies, we need gender equality, which is one of the goals for UN. That's the key.

I'm happy we can see all over the world more and more women leaders. Women are getting more and more respect. Their skills are getting acknowledged. I'm happy for it, as women roles in working societys can be also difficult. They may have lack of respect, they may be treated as an objects and not taken seriously no matter how hard workers they are with outstanding results. Women have always been fighting to gain respect. In this new errar, when people work more and more from home it gives opportunities for women to climb higher as there's not environmental pressures, there's no physical harrassment. Women entrepreneurs can have more fragile support against sexual harassment, because of lack of own working society, which would assure women rights are met correctly. In the future I hope women entrepreneurs could have some organization, which would lead women rights, where you could report about harassment. Women Entrepreneus work hard, and as every entrprepreneur they want to have collaborations, successful business partnerships, good, longlasting client relationships to secure income.

In the world where we are created as women and men. Is it possible to have gender equality? When we were created to be different in the very first moment of creation, there's no other option than to respect the differences. Only women can have the miracle of getting pregnant and giving birth for the new generations. Is it possible in the way we are created to find gender equality? Only women can carry baby in their womb for nine months, only women can breast feed the baby. But to add baby's breath to this world can only be done together, it's gender equality in the end. Needs a woman and a man. Emotional attachment is different during pregrancy, due to biological facts. How does it make fathers to feel, there can be feelings of outsider. It's important for women to carry the wisdom of emotional skills towards fathers and especially, when baby is born to let the fathers bond the same strong relationship, for building a good living foundation. Finland is forerunner for parental leave, as it has now equal parental leave for mothers and fathers. This is real gender equality and I can be proud of its development in our country.

I'm working for the betterment of humanity, for the betterment of healthcare treatments. I have been taken care of, it's my turn to help others the best way I can. And that's healthcare. I'm very happy, that my life has a meaning to help other people worldwide through Kipuwex Ltd innovative, patented medical solutions.

The UN estimates the yearly average of births between 2025 and 2030 to be 140 million. As we know children are the future, and we need to do our best to help them. For decades the medical community has been looking for an effective way of measuring pain and distress in children. Around 1,5 billion people are suffering from pain every day and 50% of doctor's visit are pain related. It is challenging to asess pain for those who are unable to communicate. Pain level is incredibly difficult to assess and currently assessment is conducted by observing the behavioral and / or physiological indicators manually from the patient and from numerous different monitoring devices. It's especially difficult to assess pain for those who are unable to communicate such as baby's, small children, individuals with mental disorders, elderly care and critical ill patients. Development of pain assessment is important because only the identified pain can be treated. Good pain management can affect many things such as relieve or suffering, reduce complications, promote patient recovery, and shorten hospitalization. It is especially important tin prematurely born babies whose neutral system is still immature. Untreated pain can cause life long trauma central nervous system, which may later lead to a disorder in development. Otherwise, acute pain should be treated as well as possible in all patients so that the pain doesn't become chronic. Chronic/prolonged pain is causing great cost to societys, not to mention human suffering.

" Only the identified pain can be treated "

Kipuwex is the first device that effectively measures pain in children using sensor data and smart algorithms. Kipuwex let's you know how much pain the baby is feeling at any moment, whether the painkillers are working and ultimately, how to treat them better.

" A baby can't tell it hurts, but Kipuwex can "

Developing countries are facing number of healthcare challenges:

-Lack of Access to Testing Labs

-Lack of affordable patient monitoring devices

-Limited amount of Medical Care Facilities

-Limited amount of healthcare professionals

-Difficult to access medical services due to poor infrastructure

Kipuwex is now launching an affordable remote monitoring device, which measures more biomarkers than any other device on the market and it's affordable to developing countries as well. Kipuwex device measures 11 different physiological parameters from the patient digitally, converting them with an algorithm into pain data and provides efficiently reliable measurements for healthcare professionals and home users. (www.kipuwex.com)

Furthermore ~20% of people worldwide are suffering from chronic pain. Kipuwex Ltd has also developed a solution for those who suffer from chronic pain (www.paincarer.com).

World needs this type of companies and affordable solutions, which promotes equality and improves people's well-being, increasing the quality of life and happiness.

Personally, I believe that the future will bring with it new technologies and solutions that will improve healthcare worldwide.

Let's respect freedom of religion or belief and work together against violence and for the betterment of healthcare, which is necessary foundation for a peaceful, prosperous and sustainable world. I have a message also to every girl, to every woman around the world. Don't let pain to stop you. You are capable to achieve your dreams. And you deserve to be happy!

CRelated links:

www.kipuwex.com

www.paincarer.com

www.happyambassador.com

14

Celebrating the Multidimensionality of Womanhood: A key Enabler of Empowerment

Rema V

Assistant Professor, Ramaiah Institute of Management, Bengaluru

Abstract *A woman has multidimensional abilities and these traits enable her to drive radical transformations. The chapter explores the core elements in a woman that facilitate in driving the change in the community and society at large. The chapter provides a glimpse of a few celebrated women from Karnataka who carry these multidimensional attributes, which are key to their empowerment and transformations brought about by them.*

Keywords: *multidimensionality, women empowerment, transformation*

Introduction

Manager, entrepreneur, athletics, pilot, artist, engineer, doctor, politician, architect, scientist to military and mining; name a profession where you cannot find a woman! That is seemingly impossible! Today, while we see successful women shining in various domains, we still hear of oppression, suppression, inequalities and discrimination.

In India, the sex ratio was 943 in 2011 to 945 in 2016 and further forecasted to increase to 948 in 2021. The sex ratio is projected to remain constant at 929 in Urban India while in rural India it is estimated to reach at 958 in 2021 from 949 in 2011. In India, the sex ratio is defined as the number of females per 1000 males in the population, A woman's average age of marriage at all India level in 2017 was 22.1 years and the same in rural and urban areas were 21.7 years and 23.1 years respectively. This parameter showed a static trend in all the major states and at all India level during the period from 2015 to 2017. The infant mortality rates have dropped over the years. The Maternal Mortality Ratio (MMR) has also seen a declining trend. During the period of 15 years from 2001-03 to 2015-17, the states of Uttar Pradesh, Assam, Rajasthan, Bihar and Madhya Pradesh have seen significantly reduced maternal mortality rate by 301 points, 261 points, 259 points, 206 points and 191 points respectively. Despite this fact these states are far above the national value of MMR at 122. In India, the literacy rate has increased to 77.7 in 2017 from 72.98 in 2011. It is observed that the male and female literacy in 2017 is at 84.7 and 70.3, respectively. The Periodic Labour Force Survey results indicate that the worker population ratio (WPR) for females in rural sector was 17.5 and 51.7 for males in 2017-18. In the urban sector, the ratio is 14.2 for females and 53.0 for males. In both rural and urban areas, WPR for females was quite lower than that of males. Further, the percentage of women representation in Central Council of Ministers has decreased from 17.8 % in 2015 to 10.5 % in 2019 [1].

What do these statistics go to tell us? While from the population statistics, the number of females has shown a positive trend, the health statistics are not very promising. Medical care has decreased mortality rates, but the numbers reveal that it is still not good enough. There is a lot more to achieve in this direction. Metrics showing the Education, Employment and participation in decision making bring to light that *'Empowerment'* still needs to transit from being a *Phenomenon* to *Reality*.

Reflections: Glimpses of the multidimensionality

There are many inspiring and empowered women who have reached the hallmarks of success. What's empowered some of them and what can be imbibed from them on one's journey towards empowerment? Indeed, there are takeaways from these *'truly empowered'* women. In this section, I will present a glimpse into some of the celebrated women with roots in Karnataka, who have sowed the seeds of inspiration and determination in me and in thousands of women like me. What helped them in reaching such levels of admirable excellence? Let's know the success stories of these empowered women..

Thimmakka, [2,3] popularly called Saalumarada Thimmakka, is an enthusiastic, die-hard environmentalist at the age 108 years, who has grown close to 400 banyan trees and protected them on a 4-km stretch between Hulikal and Kudur near Tumakuru district. *'Saalumarada'* in Kannada means rows of trees. Born in Magadi Taluk, Ramnagar, Karnataka, with no formal education, at a very young age she started working as a quarry labourer. When Thimmakka and her husband could not have any children, they decided to plant banyan saplings and raise them. She is the recipient of numerous awards including the prestigious Padma Shri in 2019. Her undying passion towards the environment and selfless service is an inspiration for generations to come. She is actively involved in numerous social and environmental campaigns, strongly driving the message of afforestation. Her work is a classic example of implementation of sustainable practices, purely driven by one's sense of commitment to the environment.

Sudha Murthy [4,5], a visionary, iconic philanthropist and an author, is known for her illustrious work for the betterment of society. Coming from Shiggaon in Karnataka, she is an engineering graduate in the 60s, which was perceived to be a degree leading to a profession not meant for women. She took to the road less travelled and was in fact the first female engineer hired by India's largest auto manufacturer TELCO. She started the Infosys Foundation in 1996. She is involved in numerous social works in the area of rural education, gender equality, public hygiene, poverty among many others. She loves teaching and publishing books. She showed that personal and professional success is possible for a woman, all it needs is determination, courage and the will. She has a large number of awards and accolades to her credit, including the prestigious Padma Shri. Indeed, she is an embodiment of simplicity, intelligence, benevolence, strength and inspiration.

Ashwini Doddalingappanavar, [6,7] a 23- year old, a symbol of courage and perseverance has driven technology-based education at Government schools in the state of Karnataka. She is instrumental in making online learning accessible to the underprivileged. She comes from a village in Kuballi, Karnataka. Ashwini has faced all the hardships in life to complete her education and join the Meghshala Trust, a non-profit organization in the domain of education, as an Implementation Associate, despite constant pressures from her parents for marriage since the age of 15 years. With hardly any money in hand, she learnt computers, English speaking and soft skills from Deshpande Foundation. She trains teachers in government schools to take online classes and has continued her support through virtual platforms even during the pandemic time. Ashwini's work has been showcased in Lenovo's New Realities Project, that gives a voice to ten empowered women driving empathy using technology amidst the pandemic times. Phil Harper, the award-winning director and producer, directed this changemaker's video for Lenovo's New Realities. She is an inspiration to the girls in her village and has been able to bring about the change in the attitude of the people in her village, for whom even the mere use of a mobile phone was considered a taboo.

While on one end we see women being as successful as their male counterparts, the society still harps on gendered jobs. Some industries and professions are assumed to be fit and dominated by a particular gender category. Jobs such as web developers, managers and drivers are largely connected with male, while teaching, cooking, nurse are among jobs associated with women. However, these trends are changing. ***Prema Nandapatti*** [8,9], called 'daredevil' by her fellow colleagues is one of the trend-setters from Karnataka who broke these 'gendered-job' stereotypes. She is the first woman driver of the Bengaluru Metropolitan Transport Corporation (BMTC). Belonging to a village near Belgaum, she was a nurse till 2009. After her husband's death, she was in dire need of a job and sought to apply at the BMTC when she could not find other opportunities. She has a no-accident record and always aligned to work ethics. A woman who believed in herself and in her abilities of taking up a profession which was deemed fit for men, is truly a source of motivation.

Kiran Mazumdar Shaw [10,11], Chairman and Managing Director of Biocon India Group, is a well-known technology pioneer and an entrepreneur. Kiran was the daughter of a brew master and wanted to pursue her goals along those lines and did a course in Melbourne University. In the 1970s, she found it hard to get a job in this field when she came back to India, because brewery was considered a 'man's job'. Challenges were numerous-gender to funding, finding people to work for her, availability of research equipment, unstable infrastructure among many others. But none of these deterred her conviction. She moved on to pursue her passion and took up a course in biotechnology. This was not a familiar field and she had to struggle it out to bring her Start up to pinnacles of success today. The Corporate Social Responsibility initiatives driven by her focus on health, infrastructure and education. She is the recipient of numerous awards including the Padma Bhushan, one of India's highest civilian honours, for being the pioneer in the biotechnology domain. Today, she is among the richest and influential women having made her mark in the field of clinical research and technology. The journey, however, wasn't easy.

Life was never rosy for all of these women. In order to '*drive the change*', they had to '*be the change*' themselves. It is their sheer passion, commitment, undying perseverance and unflinching belief in themselves, in their ability to make the difference that made them admirable and reach such levels of excellence.

The Multidimensionality of Womanhood

Women like Thimmakka, Ashwini, Prema and others are indeed testimonies of empowerment and have shown that women are capable of transforming communities and societies at large. These powerful women possess many traits which are in common. Their multidimensional attributes encompass their indomitable hard work, passion, perseverance, self-belief, education and employment which made them strong, lead from the front and drive the change [12]. The support of non-profit organizations and policy makers to women in this drive are quintessential.

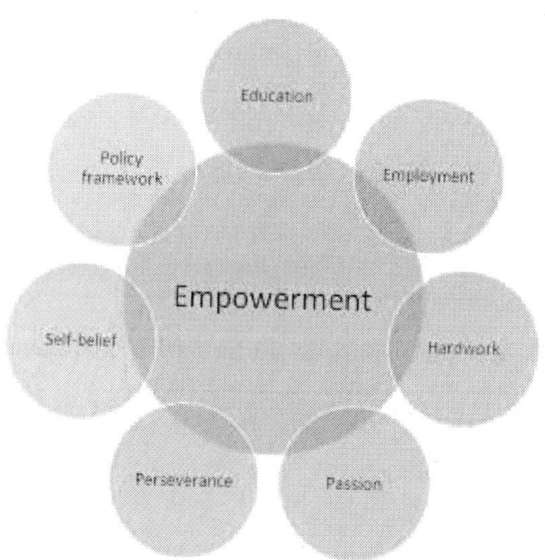

Fostering the multidimensional traits

The roots of embedding the elements of multidimensional traits lie at home. Despite being in the so-called modern and progressive era, gender inequalities and discrimination continue to exist. The transition in the mindset is the need of the hour. Celebrating the birth of a girl child is the first step.

Treating her on par with fellow male siblings, providing access to basic education, opportunities of higher education and facilitating to make her own career are significant in this direction. Shredding the tenets of patriarchal norms, giving her the freedom of expression, treating her with dignity and allowing her to be a part of decision making, starting right at home is crucial to drive confidence. The Central Government of India has launched a number of initiatives such as Beti Bachao Beti Padhao scheme, Sukanya Samriddhi Yojana, Balika Samriddhi Yojana, National Scheme of Incentive to Girls for Secondary Education etc. to enhance the social status of the girl child [13]. The efforts of the society and policy makers along this direction of enabling access to education and employment are sure to get any woman out of the cocoon and foster multitudinal traits of confidence, independence, leadership and self-belief. Let's guzzle the vibes from empowered women, work together with synergy to drive societal transformations with an attempt of breaking stereotypes and changing the mindsets.

References

[1] Women & Men in India, 2019. A statistical compilation of Gender related Indicators in India, 21st Issue. www.mospi.gov.in.

[2] 108-yr-old Saalumarada Thimmakka awarded honorary doctorate by Central Uni of Karnataka. https://www.thenewsminute.com/. 8 Nov, 2020.

[3] Saalumarada Thimmakka, A Century Old Environmentalist. https://blog.bitsathy.ac.in/. 13 Sep, 2019.

[4] Sudha Murthy- An Iconic Women, Philanthropist, and Author. https://www.karnataka.com/personalities/sudha-murty/. 1 Dec, 2016.

[5] Sudha Murthy- An idol and a superstar for millions and trillions. https://www.finnovationz.com/blog/.

[6] Women Educators Working in Underprivileged Communities. https://leverageedu.com/blog/ . 7 Nov, 2020.

[7] Meet the young changemaker who is driving tech-driven education in government schools in Karnataka. https://yourstory.com/herstory/2020/10/. 20 Oct, 2020.

[8] Women achievers of Karnataka. https://metrosaga.com/. 7 Mar, 2019.

[9] Prema Ramappa. http://blog.urbantreehomes.com/about-prema-ramappa/. 30 Mar, 2016.

[10] Kiran Mazumdar Shaw. https://www.britannica.com/biography/.

[11] The journey of Kiran Mazumdar Shaw. https://www.startupstories.in/stories/inspirational-stories/

[12] Williams, J. (2005). Measuring gender and women's empowerment using confirmatory factor analysis. *Population Program, Institute of Behavioural Science, University of Colorado, Boulder.*

[13] Top 5 Central Government Girl Child Schemes In India. https://www.goodreturns.in/personal-finance/investment/. 7 Sep, 2020.

15

Professionalism, being Goodwill Ambassador and Empowerment

Denisa Gokovi

Model/ Actress/ Writer Albania

Global Goodwill Ambassador

Professional integrity is the choice that makes the difference in our purpose. The way to realize our efforts is to strengthen the requirements and objectives. Our attitude is important to be united. Collaboration is part of the elements of how we cultivate our future. Choosing people who understand your individuality is professional courage. In negotiations to act confidently, there is always the opportunity to reflect it in different directions. This is called multifaceted relationships for the right results. Self-confidence is the balancing force to guide your goals with vision and great influence. When we have managed to form the audience with the improvement of ideas, we have achieved the intermediate goal of success. In the global cause, we all strive for the same things, but we have not understood that competition has no level, but the individual level leads the concept that develops important opportunities. We must insist on the favors that are created in the work model by opposing the wrong priorities and discussing the active reflection of the people. The inclusion of many issues to strengthen human relationships lies in the secret of ambition to change the essence of the human objective. Dedication and the need to share things with others shows the exploratory power in global unity to achieve success. Being yourself like an Ambassador too is a great social responsibility starting with the way of thinking, protecting and the efficiency of certain changes in the improvement of people's lives, the civilization of new ideas and the possible changes in different representations. Of course, there are different categories of ambassadors' roles, and not all of them belong to a pure market in terms of diplomatic goals. In this sense, the views are divided into political categories and the image is conveyed by an Ambassador. The most obvious challenge is the effort to spread global unity in leading human well-being and structuring survival, including the implementation of human rights, gender equality, and non-political or religious mentality. Ambassador of Peace, of goodwill or of culture and art as I have represented is part of the merits of a bridge of cooperation for constructive and communicative knowledge and foundations in humanity by promising broad social responsibility and awareness on a human scale. To be an Ambassador means that you are yourself in two powers must be perfect to complement each other. Inspirational culture and dominant spirit.

The passion for being oneself brings with it ways of improving oneself. Shows ingenuity and self-confidence. Any other attempt is temporary. The qualities of a personality reinforce the inner thought in man to realize that great changes come if you stay in your abyss without any conditions. To secure our position, we need to lead ourselves before sharing it with others. Life conflict is the cause of understanding passive mistakes and the energy that mediates the passion to win is directly related to our needs and ourselves. It all starts to understand that the importance of others should be you.

Success is the highest feeling that does not deserve compromise and this is related to individual integrity. What we represent is the safe destination of new challenges.

Encouragement in the most difficult conditions is really important and the inner strength to make big changes. Professional goals are related to your identity and skills. How can we believe that anything can be accomplished? Through the price of patience and the structures that must be followed with vigilance. No one can be intimidated by the prejudices based on the possibility that they are created through the will and power that we share with people as they support us to find themselves in us.

There are several reasons that can hinder the stability of our ideas and they are more related to unnecessary commitments. The focus is on the programmed strategy that should support the main balances of a critical outcome such as the career itself.

the morale of your professional position that shows the experience of each of us, shows a lot of difficulties and sacrifices that we cultivate with determination.

It is very important that professional goals and individual integrity, considering passion itself, organizes human creativity, where it brings us to the priority of contributing to society and this is called true success.

The experience of each of us has shown ups and downs, showing that vigilance remains a concept that must be sustained. The world is a cause in itself and cannot be changed by those who do not defend themselves by trying. The most important issues are a balanced rule to encourage primitive secrets in attempts to save people from social rather than innovative pressure. There are many countries that suffer from prejudice and many reasons that indicate unnecessary limits. The reason for being you is individual power, so everything is related to the integrity of thought, producing time through human co-operation.

16

Women Empowerment in India How do Suffer in Life

Sandhya Singh[1], Neeraj Pathak[2], Sunil Kumar[3]

Department of Management, Rajiv Academy for Technology & Management, GLA University Mathura, UP, India

Abstract: India is a traditional country and there is diversity in religions, culture and customs. Role of the women in India mostly is household and limited to domestic issues. In some cases women can find employment as nurses, doctors, teachers the caring and nurturing sectors. But even if well qualified women engineers or managers or geologists are available, preference will be given to a male of equal qualification.

The present study investigated to identify the factors preventing women employees from aspiring for higher post and challenges & problems faced by women workers. Further the study try to explain the real condition of Indian working women and also make an effort to clear main problems of working women.

Keywords: challenges, problems, traditional, women workers

INTRODUCTION

"Gender Equality means that women and men have equal conditions for realizing their full human rights and potential to contribute to national, political, economic social and cultural development and benefit equally from the results..... Attaining gender equality demands recognition that current social, economic, cultural, and political systems are gendered; that women's equal status is systematic and that is necessary to incorporate women's specificity priorities and values into all major social institutions." In the last three decades, women who make up half of the world's population have benefited more than men from progress in social and economic development. But this is not true in India as India shows disproportionate sex ratio. Though India is marching forward to the status of developed nation, it is shocking to find that population of females has been comparatively lower than males. In spite of, they continue to be over represented among the world's most vulnerable groups, as access to some resources and power remains highly skewed towards men. There are always a number of components in the society which are disregarded of their basic rights in every society, state and nation, but these components lack in the awareness of their rights. If we enlist such components from the society, then women would must be top this list. In fact, all women are the important factor of every society. Gender equality is the process of being fair to women and men. It is a goal in its own right but also a key factor for sustainable social development, economic growth and environmental sustainability. A sustainable path of development can be achieved to ensure that women's and men's interests are both taken into account in the allocation of resources through providing the same opportunities to men and women. Basically, equality between women and men should be promoted in ways that are appropriate to each particular context. Both men and women have a stake building a more just society where all people are equally valued for their contributions. In 1992, the United Nations Conference on Environmental Development (UNCED) made important provisions for the recognition of women's contribution and their full participation in sustainable development.

The United Nations has accepted 17 Sustainable Development Goals (SDGs) with specific targets to achieve within stipulated time. The common goal of SDGs that no one will be left behind is a move towards equitable and inclusive society for all. It is only for to end the poverty and ensure that people enjoy with fruitful peace and prosper. The Concept of Sustainable Development and Goals . In the late 1980s the report of Our Common Future by the World Commission on Environment and Development defined the concept of "Sustainable Development" as development which "meets the needs of the present without compromising the ability of future generations to meet their own needs".

What is meant by Women's Empowerment?

Based on the assumptions that women differ from men in their social positions and that those differences consist of asymmetric, unequal power relations between the genders, "women's empowerment" refers to the process of increasing women's access to control over the strategic life choices that affect them and access to the opportunities that allow them fully to realize their capacities.

As per **Keshab Chandra Mandal** female empowerment could be defined in five separate categories: social, educational, economic, political, and psychological. Social empowerment might be one of the most prominent forms of empowerment shown in the mainstream media. It strengthens women's social relations and their positions in social structures, giving them more of a purpose outside of the home.

Equality of access to and attainment of educational qualifications is necessary if more women are to become agents of change. Literacy of women is an important key to improving health, nutrition and education in the family and to empowering women to participate in decision-making in society..

OBJECTIVE OF THE STUDY

1. To identify the factors preventing women employees from aspiring for higher post and challenges & problems faced by women workers.

2. To clear main problems of working women.

There are "3Ls" of women empowerment which includes

- **learning,**
- **labour and**
- **leadership.**

Learning helps women to get limitless knowledge which helps them to broaden their thoughts. It helps women to overcome adversities. According to Mahatma Gandhi, "If you educate a man you educate an individual, but if you educate a woman you educate an entire family." There is a famous African adage: "If you educate a boy, you train a man. If you educate a girl, you train a village."

Empowerment, Women's Empowerment and Human Rights

- **Empowerment** – – –Empowerment is a multi-dimensional process which should enable individuals or a group of individuals to realize their full identity and powers in all spheres of life. According to Webster dictionary the word empowerment indicates the situation of authority or to be authorized or to powerful.

- **Women's Empowerment** – -Women empowerment means emancipation of women from the vicious grips of social, economic, political, caste and gender based discrimination. It means granting women freedom to make life choices. It can also be seen as an important process in reaching gender equality, which means "rights, responsibilities and opportunities of individuals will not depend on whether they are born male or female". Women empowerment itself elaborates the social rights, political rights, economic stability and all other rights should be also equal to women. Basically empowerment is an essential which can help women to achieve equality with men or to reduce gender gap considerably (P.K.B Nayar). Specifically the concept of empowerment for women flows from the power. Indeed empowerment of women focuses on enabling women to be economically independent and self reliant. According to United Nations would survey (2014) on the "Role of Women in Development 2014" there are proven synergies between women's empowerment and economic, social and environmental sustainability. The empowered women should be able to take part in the process of decision making in every possible level. If women get recognition from the society for their latent talents, skills and leadership abilities, there will not be ant conflict and violation of human rights. Gender equality is both an essential element of any development process and a result of sustainable development process and a result of sustainable development. Development efforts should not only aim to advance equality between women and men as an outcome, but should also advance equality throughout by applying gender analysis in planning, consultations, design, implementations and assessment. It is one of the goals of Millennium Development which proposes to eliminate gender disparity in primary and secondary education, preferably by 2005, and all levels of education no later than 2015. The Indicators for Achievement of Millennium Development Goal 4 are Equality in: • Ratio of girls to boys in primary, secondary, and tertiary education. • Ratio of literate women to men ages 15 to 24. • Share of women in wage employment in the non-agricultural sector. • Proportion of seats held by women in National Parliament.

- **Human Rights** The "rights responsibilities and opportunities of individuals will not depend on whether they are born male or female". Human rights are generally understood as being those rights that are intrinsic to all human beings. The concept of human rights acknowledges that each individual is entitled to exercise his or her rights without any forms of discrimination regarding areas such as caste, creed, race, gender, language, religion, political or property, birth, background and status. Nevertheless the Gender Action Plan 2016-2020 recognizes that gender equality is a matter of human rights, the foundation of democracy and good governance, sustainable development. It acknowledges the underpinnings of gender inequality, namely the unequal gender power relations and gender biased social norms that discriminate against women and girls, marginalizing them from the benefits of social, economic and political change.

Gender and Gender Equality vs. Gender Equity

- **Gender—-** Gender is not something we are born with, and not something we have, but something we do (West and Zimmerman), but something we perform (Butler 1990). Basically gender refers to the social differences and relations between men and women. This refers to socially and culturally ascribed roles to men and women. Gender roles are learned behaviors. The term gender does not replace the term sex. Sex is a biological categorization based primarily on reproductive potential, whereas gender is the social elaboration of biological sex. So, gender roles are affected by age, class, race, ethnicity, religion and by economic and political environment.

- **Gender Equality** The concept of gender equality is since long established as the preferred working for equal rights, life prospects, opportunities and power for women and men, girls and boys. It is used in all key international agreements, from the Convention on the Elimination of All Forms of Discrimination Against Women (CEDAW) in 1979 to the Sustainable Development Goals in 2015. Gender equality is a concept with transformative connotation, covering women's empowerment, non discrimination and equal rights regardless of gender. It embraces multi-dimensional view on inequalities between women and men, girls and boys.

- **Gender Equity** --Gender equity means fairness of treatment for women and men, according to their respective needs. Equity is used for example within the education, health and humanitarian sectors referring to the equal distribution of resources based on the needs of different groups of people. Gender equity in this context refers to the fact that a gender analysis of these needs is necessary, as they in many respects may be different for women and men, boys and girls. When used in this way the concept gender equity has opened up for a definition that only embraces part of the gender equality agenda. Thus it leaves the transformative and challenging aspects of gender equality out and makes it possible to avoid the necessary contestation of power relations and unequal social, economic and political structures.

Empowering women for Sustainable development-- Sustainable development cannot achieve without gender equality. It also depends on an equitable distribution of resources. Women's empowerment is a multi-dimensional process and it is a key factor for achieving sustainable economic growth, social development and environmental sustainability. So far gender issues have been primarily dealt with as a social issue. Moreover, in all countries women are sharing the primary responsibility for nutrition and household management. In most developing countries, women play a vital role like farmers, water and fuel collectors. Women took much essential achieve part in the Rio Earth Summit process and succeeded in obtaining a chapter on women and sustainable development. The 1992 summit, together with the 1993 Human Rights Conference, the 1994 International Conference on Population and Development, the 1995 Social Summit and the 1995 Fourth World Conference on Women, have focused the work of the United Nations on the environment, population, human rights, poverty and gender. UNDP coordinates global and national efforts to integrate gender equality and women's empowerment into poverty reduction, crisis prevention and recovery, democratic governance and sustainable development. The Fourth World Conference on Women held in Beijing in September 1995, emphasized that empowerment full participation and equality for women are the foundations for peace and sustainable development.

Role of Education for Sustainable Development The importance of gender equality in achieving the right to education for all has been recognized. A transformative education agenda should include 'inclusion and equity' in and through education. "The Incheon Declaration rightly commits us to non discriminatory education that recognizes the importance of gender equality and women's empowerment for sustainable development. This is a crucial opportunity for us to work together, across sectors, towards the fulfilment of the education for all promise of peaceful, just and equal societies. A world where people are equal can only be achieved if our education also university teacher this." -Phumzile Mlambo-Ngcuka, UN Women Executive Director Commitment had been shown to develop gender sensitive policies, mainstreaming gender issues in teacher training and eliminating gender based discrimination in schools. UN World Survey on "Role of Women in Development 2014" as female education level rise, child morality rates fall and family health improves. So, education also increases women's participation in the welfare society as decision maker, labor force in various work places and their contribution to household and national economic growth.

The General Assembly adopted 2030 agenda for Sustainable Development that includes 17 Sustainable Development Goals and 169 targets to realize the human rights of all and to achieve gender equality and the empowerment of all women and gi=rls. These 17 Goals build on the success of the Millennium Development Goals that emphasized only equality of opportunity and the 2030 (SDGs) agenda acknowledges that equality must be based on both opportunity and outcome.

The 17 points should be in india:

1. End hunger, achieve food security and improved nutrition and promote sustainable agriculture
2. End poverty in all its forms everywhere
3. Ensure healthy lives and promote well-being for all at all ages
4. Ensure inclusive and equitable quality education and promote lifelong learning opportunities for all.
5. Achieve gender equality and empower all women and girls.
6. .Ensure availability and sustainable management of water and sanitation for all .
7. Ensure access to affordable, reliable, sustainable and modern energy for all
8. Promote sustained, inclusive and sustainable economic growth, full and productive employment and decent work for all .
9. Build resilient infrastructure, promote inclusive and sustainable industrialization and foster innovation.
10. Reduce inequality within and among countries
11. Make cities and human settlements inclusive, safe, resilient and sustainable.
12. Ensure sustainable consumption and production .
13. Take urgent action to combat climate change and its impacts.
14. Conserve and sustainability use the oceans, seas and marine resources for sustainable development.
15. Protect, restore and promote sustainable use of terrestrial ecosystems, sustainably manage forests,

combat desertification, and halt and reverse land degradation and halt biodiversity loss.

16. Promote peaceful and inclusive societies for sustainable development, provide access to justice for all and build effective, accountable and inclusive institutions at all levels

17. .Strengthen the means of implementation and revitalize the global partnership for sustainable .

Gender equality in India

Ending all discrimination against women and girls is not only a basic human right, it's crucial for sustainable future; it's proven that empowering women and girls helps economic growth and development.

UNDP has made gender equality central to its work and we've seen remarkable progress in the past 20 years. There are more girls in school now compared to 15 years ago, and most regions have reached gender parity in primary education.

But although there are more women than ever in the labour market, there are still large inequalities in some regions, with women systematically denied the same work rights as men. Sexual violence and exploitation, the unequal division of unpaid care and domestic work, and discrimination in public office all remain huge barriers. Climate change and disasters continue to have a disproportionate effect on women and children, as do conflict and migration.

It is vital to give women equal rights land and property, sexual and reproductive health, and to technology and the internet. Today there are more women in public office than ever before, but encouraging more women leaders will help achieve greater gender equality.

NATIONAL POLICY FOR THE EMPOWERMENT OF WOMEN (2001)

Introduction

The principle of gender equality is enshrined in the Indian Constitution in its Preamble, Fundamental Rights, Fundamental Duties and Directive Principles. The Constitution not only grants equality to women, but also empowers the State to adopt measures of positive discrimination in favour of women.

Within the framework of a democratic polity, our laws, development policies, Plans and programmes have aimed at women's advancement in different spheres. From the Fifth Five Year Plan (1974-78) onwards has been a marked shift in the approach to women's issues from welfare to development. In recent years, the empowerment of women has been recognized as the central issue in determining the status of women. The National Commission for Women was set up by an Act of Parliament in 1990 to safeguard the rights and legal entitlements of women. The 73rd and 74th Amendments (1993) to the Constitution of India have provided for reservation of seats in the local bodies of Panchayats and Municipalities for women, laying a strong foundation for their participation in decision making at the local levels.

- India has also ratified various international conventions and human rights instruments committing to secure equal rights of women. Key among them is the ratification of the Convention on Elimination of All Forms of Discrimination Against Women (CEDAW) in 1993..
- The Policy also takes note of the commitments of the Ninth Five Year Plan and the other Sectoral Policies relating to empowerment of Women.
- The women's movement and a wide-spread network of non-Government Organisations which have strong grass-roots presence and deep insight into women's

concerns have contributed in inspiring initiatives for the empowerment of women.

- However, there still exists a wide gap between the goals enunciated in the Constitution, legislation, policies, plans, programmes, and related mechanisms on the one hand and the situational reality of the status of women in India, on the other. This has been analyzed extensively in the Report of the Committee on the Status of Women in India, "Towards Equality", 1974 and highlighted in the National Perspective Plan for Women, 1988-2000, the Shramshakti Report, 1988 and the Platform for Action, Five Years After- An assessment"

- Gender disparity manifests itself in various forms, the most obvious being the trend of continuously declining female ratio in the population in the last few decades. Social stereotyping and violence at the domestic and societal levels are some of the other manifestations. Discrimination against girl children, adolescent girls and women persists in parts of the country.

- The underlying causes of gender inequality are related to social and economic structure, which is based on informal and formal norms, and practices.

- Consequently, the access of women particularly those belonging to weaker sections including Scheduled Castes/Scheduled Tribes/ Other backward Classes and minorities, majority of whom are in the rural areas and in the informal, unorganized sector – to education, health and productive resources, among others, is inadequate. Therefore, they remain largely marginalized, poor and socially excluded.

Goal

1. The goal of this Policy is to bring about the advancement, development and empowerment of

women. The Policy will be widely disseminated so as to encourage active participation of all stakeholders for achieving its goals. Specifically, the objectives of this Policy include

(i) Creating an environment through positive economic and social policies for full development of women to enable them to realize their full potential

(ii) The de-jure and de-facto enjoyment of all human rights and fundamental freedom by women on equal basis with men in all spheres - political, economic, social, cultural and civil

(iii) Equal access to participation and decision making of women in social, political and economic life of the nation

(iv) Equal access to women to health care, quality education at all levels, career and vocational guidance, employment, equal remuneration, occupational health and safety, social security and public office etc.

(v) Strengthening legal systems aimed at elimination of all forms of discrimination against women

(vi) Changing societal attitudes and community practices by active participation and involvement of both men and women.

(vii) Mainstreaming a gender perspective in the development process.

(viii) Elimination of discrimination and all forms of violence against women and the girl child; and

(ix) Building and strengthening partnerships with civil society, particularly women's organizations.

PolicyPrescriptions

Judicial Legal Systems

Legal-judicial system will be made more responsive and gender sensitive to women's needs, especially in cases of domestic violence and personal assault. New laws will be enacted and existing laws reviewed to ensure that justice is quick and the punishment meted out to the culprits is commensurate with the severity of the offence.

- At the initiative of and with the full participation of all stakeholders including community and religious leaders, the Policy would aim to encourage changes in personal laws such as those related to marriage, divorce, maintenance and guardianship so as to eliminate discrimination against women.
- The evolution of property rights in a patriarchal system has contributed to the subordinate status of women. The Policy would aim to encourage changes in laws relating to ownership of property and inheritance by evolving consensus in order to make them gender just.

Decision Making

Women's equality in power sharing and active participation in decision making, including decision making in political process at all levels will be ensured for the achievement of the goals of empowerment. All measures will be taken to guarantee women equal access to and full participation in decision making bodies at every level, including the legislative, executive, judicial, corporate, statutory bodies, as also the advisory Commissions, Committees, Boards, Trusts etc. Affirmative action such as reservations/quotas, including in higher legislative bodies, will be considered whenever necessary on a time bound basis. Women-friendly personnel policies will also be drawn up to encourage women to participate effectively in the developmental process.

Mainstreaming a Gender Perspective in the Development Process

Policies, programmes and systems will be established to ensure mainstreaming of women's perspectives in all developmental processes, as catalysts, participants and recipients. Wherever there are gaps in policies and programmes, women specific interventions would be undertaken to bridge these. Coordinating and monitoring mechanisms will also be devised to assess from time to time the progress of such mainstreaming mechanisms. Women's issues and concerns as a result will specially be addressed and reflected in all concerned laws, sectoral policies, plans and programmes of action.

Economic Empowerment of women

Poverty Eradication

Since women comprise the majority of the population below the poverty line and are very often in situations of extreme poverty, given the harsh realities of intra-household and social discrimination, macro economic policies and poverty eradication programmes will specifically address the needs and problems of such women. There will be improved implementation of programmes which are already women oriented with special targets for women. Steps will be taken for mobilization of poor women and convergence of services, by offering them a range of economic and social options, along with necessary support measures to enhance their capabilities

Micro Credit

In order to enhance women's access to credit for consumption and production, the establishment of new, and strengthening of existing micro-credit mechanisms and micro-finance institution will be undertaken so that the outreach of credit is enhanced. Other supportive measures would be taken to ensure adequate flow of credit through extant financial institutions and banks, so that all women below poverty line have easy access to credit.

Women and Economy

Women's perspectives will be included in designing and implementing macro-economic and social policies by institutionalizing their participation in such processes. Their contribution to socio-economic development as producers and workers will be recognized in the formal and informal sectors (including home based workers) and appropriate policies relating to employment and to her working conditions will be drawn up. Such measures could include:

Reinterpretation and redefinition of conventional concepts of work wherever necessary e.g. in the Census records, to reflect women's contribution as producers and workers.

Globalization

Globalization has presented new challenges for the realization of the goal of women's equality, the gender impact of which has not been systematically evaluated fully. However, from the micro-level studies that were commissioned by the Department of Women & Child Development, it is evident that there is a need for re-framing policies for access to employment and quality of employment. Benefits of the growing global economy have been unevenly distributed leading to wider economic disparities, the feminization of poverty, increased gender inequality through often deteriorating working conditions and unsafe working environment especially in the informal economy and rural areas. Strategies will be designed to enhance the capacity of women and empower them to meet the negative social and economic impacts, which may flow from the globalization process.

Women and Agriculture

In view of the critical role of women in the agriculture and allied sectors, as producers, concentrated efforts will be made to ensure that benefits of training, extension and various programmes will reach them in proportion to their numbers. The programmes for training women in soil conservation, social forestry, dairy development and other occupations allied to agriculture like horticulture, livestock including small animal husbandry, poultry, fisheries etc. will be expanded to benefit women workers in the agriculture sector.

Women and Industry

The important role played by women in electronics, information technology and food processing and agro industry and textiles has been crucial to the development of these sectors. They would be given comprehensive support in terms of labour legislation, social security and other support services to participate in various industrial sectors.

Women at present cannot work in night shift in factories even if they wish to. Suitable measures will be taken to enable women to work on the night shift in factories. This will be accompanied with support services for security, transportation etc.

Support Services

The provision of support services for women, like child care facilities, including crèches at work places and educational institutions, homes for the aged and the disabled will be expanded and improved to create an enabling environment and to ensure their full cooperation in social, political and economic life. Women-friendly personnel policies will also be drawn up to encourage women to participate effectively in the developmental process.

Social Empowerment of Women

Education

Equal access to education for women and girls will be ensured. Special measures will be taken to eliminate discrimination, universalize education, eradicate illiteracy, create a gender-sensitive educational system, increase enrolment and retention rates of girls and improve the quality of education to facilitate life-long learning as well as development of occupation/vocation/technical skills by women. Reducing the gender gap in secondary and higher education would be a focus area. Sectoral time targets in existing policies will be achieved, with a special focus on girls and women, particularly those belonging to weaker sections including the Scheduled Castes/Scheduled Tribes/Other Backward Classes/Minorities. Gender sensitive curricula would be developed at all levels of educational system in order to address sex stereotyping as one of the causes of gender discrimination.

Health

A holistic approach to women's health which includes both nutrition and health services will be adopted and special attention will be given to the needs of women and the girl at all stages of the life cycle. The reduction of infant mortality and maternal mortality, which are sensitive indicators of human development, is a priority concern. This policy reiterates the national demographic goals for Infant Mortality Rate (IMR), Maternal Mortality Rate (MMR) set out in the National Population Policy 2000. Women should have access to comprehensive, affordable and quality health care. Measures will be adopted that take into account the reproductive rights of women to enable them to exercise informed choices, their vulnerability to sexual and health problems together with endemic, infectious and communicable diseases such as malaria, TB, and water borne diseases as well as hypertension and cardio-pulmonary diseases. The social, developmental and health consequences of HIV/AIDS and other sexually transmitted diseases will be tackled from a gender perspective.

To effectively meet problems of infant and maternal mortality, and early marriage the availability of good and accurate data at micro level on deaths, birth and marriages is required. Strict implementation of registration of births and deaths would be ensured and registration of marriages would be made compulsory.

- In accordance with the commitment of the National Population Policy (2000) to population stabilization, this Policy recognizes the critical need of men and women to have access to safe, effective and affordable methods of family planning of their choice and the need to suitably address the issues of early marriages and spacing of children. Interventions such as spread of education, compulsory registration of marriage and special programmes like BSY should impact on delaying the age of marriage so that by 2010 child marriages are eliminated.

- Women's traditional knowledge about health care and nutrition will be recognized through proper documentation and its use will be encouraged. The use of Indian and alternative systems of medicine will be enhanced within the framework of overall health infrastructure available for women.

Nutrition

In view of the high risk of malnutrition and disease that women face at all the three critical stages viz., infancy and childhood, adolescent and reproductive phase, focussed attention would be paid to meeting the nutritional needs of women at all stages of the life cycle. This is also important in view of the critical link between the health of adolescent girls, pregnant and lactating women with the health of infant and young children. Special efforts will be made to tackle the problem of macro and micro nutrient deficiencies especially amongst pregnant and lactating women as it leads to various diseases and disabilities.

- Intra-household discrimination in nutritional matters vis-à-vis girls and women will be sought to be ended through appropriate strategies. Widespread use of nutrition education would be made to address the issues of intra-household imbalances in nutrition and the special needs of pregnant and lactating women.

Women's participation will also be ensured in the planning, superintendence and delivery of the system.

Drinking Water and Sanitation

Special attention will be given to the needs of women in the provision of safe drinking water, sewage disposal, toilet facilities and sanitation within accessible reach of households, especially in rural areas and urban slums. Women's participation will be ensured in the planning, delivery and maintenance of such services.

Housing and Shelter

Women's perspectives will be included in housing policies, planning of housing colonies and provision of shelter both in rural and urban areas. Special attention will be given for providing adequate and safe housing and accommodation for women including single women, heads of households, working women, students, apprentices and trainees.

Environment

Women will be involved and their perspectives reflected in the policies and programmes for environment, conservation and restoration. Considering the impact of environmental factors on their livelihoods, women's participation will be ensured in the conservation of the environment and control of environmental degradation. The vast majority of rural women still depend on the locally available non-commercial sources of energy such as animal dung, crop waste and fuel wood. In order to ensure the efficient use of these energy resources in an environmental friendly manner, the Policy will aim at promoting the programmes of non-conventional energy resources. Women will be involved in spreading the use of solar energy, biogas, smokeless chulahs and other rural application so as to have a visible impact of these measures in influencing eco system and in changing the life styles of rural women.

Science and Technology

Programmes will be strengthened to bring about a greater involvement of women in science and technology. These will include measures to motivate girls to take up science and technology for higher education and also ensure that development projects with scientific and technical inputs involve women fully. Efforts to develop a scientific temper and awareness will also be stepped up. Special measures would be taken for their training in areas where they have special skills like communication and information technology. Efforts to develop appropriate technologies suited to women's needs as well as to reduce their drudgery will be given a special focus too.

Women in Difficult Circumstances

In recognition of the diversity of women's situations and in acknowledgement of the needs of specially disadvantaged groups, measures and programmes will be undertaken to provide them with special assistance. These groups include women in extreme poverty, destitute women, women in conflict situations, women affected by natural calamities, women in less developed regions, the disabled widows, elderly women, single women in difficult circumstances, women heading households, those displaced from employment, migrants, women who are victims of marital violence, deserted women and prostitutes etc.

Violence against women

All forms of violence against women, physical and mental, whether at domestic or societal levels, including those arising from customs, traditions or accepted practices shall be dealt with effectively with a view to eliminate its incidence. Institutions and mechanisms/schemes for assistance will be created and strengthened for prevention of such violence , including sexual harassment at work place and customs like dowry; for the rehabilitation of the victims of violence and for taking effective action against the perpetrators of such

will be strengthened. These will be through interventions as may be appropriate and will relate to, among others, provision of adequate resources, training and advocacy skills to effectively influence macro-policies, legislation, programmes etc. to achieve the empowerment of women.

- National and State Councils will be formed to oversee the operationalisation of the Policy on a regular basis. The National Council will be headed by the Prime Minister and the State Councils by the Chief Ministers and be broad in composition having representatives from the concerned Departments/Ministries, National and State Commissions for Women, Social Welfare Boards, representatives of Non-Government Organizations, Women's Organisations, Corporate Sector, Trade Unions, financing institutions, academics, experts and social activists etc. These bodies will review the progress made in implementing the Policy twice a year. The National Development Council will also be informed of the progress of the programme undertaken under the policy from time to time for advice and comments.

- National and State Resource Centres on women will be established with mandates for collection and dissemination of information, undertaking research work, conducting surveys, implementing training and awareness generation programmes, etc. These Centers will link up with Women's Studies Centres and other research and academic institutions through suitable information networking systems.

- While institutions at the district level will be strengthened, at the grass-roots, women will be helped by Government through its programmes to organize and strengthen into Self-Help Groups (SHGs) at the Anganwadi/Village/Town level. The women's groups will be helped to institutionalize themselves into registered societies and to federate at the Panchyat/ Municipal level. These societies will bring about synergistic implementation of all the social and economic development programmes by drawing resources made available through Government and Non-Government channels, including banks and financial institutions and by establishing a close Interface with the Panchayats/ Municipalities.

Resource Management

- Availability of adequate financial, human and market resources to implement the Policy will be managed by concerned Departments, financial credit institutions and banks, private sector, civil society and other connected institutions. This process will include:

(a) Assessment of benefits flowing to women and resource allocation to the programmes relating to them through an exercise of gender budgeting. Appropriate changes in policies will be made to optimize benefits to women under these schemes;

(b) Adequate resource allocation to develop and promote the policy outlined earlier based on above by concerned Departments.

(c) Developing synergy between personnel of Health, Rural Development, Education and Women & Child Development Department at field level and other village level functionaries'

(d) Meeting credit needs by banks and financial credit institutions through suitable policy initiatives and development of new institutions in coordination with the Department of Women & Child Development.

- The strategy of Women's Component Plan adopted in the Ninth Plan of ensuring that not less than 30% of benefits/funds flow to women from all Ministries and Departments will be implemented effectively so that the needs and interests of women and girls are addressed by all concerned sectors. The Department of Women and Child Development being the nodal Ministry will monitor and review the progress of the implementation of the Component Plan from time to time, in terms of both quality and quantity in collaboration with the Planning Commission.

- Efforts will be made to channelize private sector investments too, to support programmes and projects for advancement of women

Legislation

- The existing legislative structure will be reviewed and additional legislative measures taken by identified departments to implement the Policy. This will also involve a review of all existing laws including personal, customary and tribal laws, subordinate legislation, related rules as well as executive and administrative regulations to eliminate all gender discriminatory references. The process will be planned over a time period 2000-2003. The specific measures required would be evolved through a consultation process involving civil society, National Commission for Women and Department of Women and Child Development. In appropriate cases the consultation process would be widened to include other stakeholders too.
- Effective implementation of legislation would be promoted by involving civil society and community. Appropriate changes in legislation will be undertaken, if necessary.
- In addition, following other specific measures will be taken to implement the legislation effectively.

(a) Strict enforcement of all relevant legal provisions and speedy redressed of grievances will be ensured, with a special focus on violence and gender related atrocities.

(b) Measures to prevent and punish sexual harassment at the place of work, protection for women workers in the organized/ unorganized sector and strict enforcement of relevant laws such as Equal Remuneration Act and Minimum Wages Act will be undertaken,

(c) Crimes against women, their incidence, prevention, investigation, detection and prosecution will be regularly reviewed at all Crime Review fora and Conferences at the Central, State and District levels. Recognised, local, voluntary organizations will be authorized to lodge Complaints and facilitate registration, investigations and legal proceedings related to violence and atrocities against girls and women.

(d) Women's Cells in Police Stations, Encourage Women Police Stations Family Courts, Mahila Courts, Counselling Centers, Legal Aid Centers and Nyaya Panchayats will be strengthened and expanded to eliminate violence and atrocities against women.

(e) Widespread dissemination of information on all aspects of legal rights, human rights and other entitlements of women, through specially designed legal literacy programmes and rights information programmes will be done.

Gender Sensitization

- Training of personnel of executive, legislative and judicial wings of the State, with a special focus on policy and programme framers, implementation and development agencies, law enforcement machinery and the judiciary, as well as non-governmental organizations will be undertaken. Other measures will include:

(a) Promoting societal awareness to gender issues and women's human rights.

(b) Review of curriculum and educational materials to include gender education and human rights issues

(c) Removal of all references derogatory to the dignity of women from all public documents and legal instruments.

(d) Use of different forms of mass media to communicate social messages relating to women's equality and empowerment.

Panchayati Raj Institutions

- The 73rd and 74th Amendments (1993) to the Indian Constitution have served as a breakthrough towards ensuring equal access and increased participation in political power structure for women. The PRIs will play a central role in the process of enhancing women's participation in public life. The PRIs and the local self Governments will be actively involved in the implementation and execution of the National Policy for Women at the grassroots level.

Partnership with the voluntary sector organizations

- The involvement of voluntary organizations, associations, federations, trade unions, non-governmental organizations, women's organizations, as well as institutions dealing with education, training and research will be ensured in the formulation, implementation, monitoring and review of all policies and programmes affecting women. Towards this end, they will be provided with appropriate support related to resources and capacity building and facilitated to participate actively in the process of the empowerment of women.

International Cooperation

- The Policy will aim at implementation of international obligations/commitments in all sectors on empowerment of women such as the Convention on All Forms of Discrimination Against Women (CEDAW), Convention on the Rights of the Child (CRC), International Conference on Population and Development (ICPD+5) and other such instruments. International, regional and sub-regional cooperation towards the empowerment of women will continue to be encouraged through sharing of experiences, exchange of ideas and technology, networking with institutions and organizations and through bilateral and multi-lateral partnerships.

Six ways the government is pushing for women's empowerment in India

This Independence Day, we take a look at various schemes initiated by the government for women's empowerment in India. These range from community engagement and welfare of the girl child to women's safety and more.

For an Indian woman and citizen, freedom does not just mean those guaranteed under the Constitution. It also means more jobs, opportunities for entrepreneurship, increased safety, ease in day-to-day living, and protection of the girl child. In short, the road to women's empowerment has several factors dotting its path

To ensure women are empowered, the government and the public sector need to play important roles to enable their welfare in various sectors. Whether it's providing free cooking gas and education schemes or enabling women to leverage technology, a slew of schemes has been launched in recent years to empower women to be independent in their lives.

Here are a few that are breaking new ground and improving the lives of women, and encouraging them to think big, both in urban and rural areas.

1. **Beti Bachao Beti Padhao Yojana Launched on January 22, 2015**, in Panipat, Haryana, it aims to generate

awareness and also improve the efficiency of welfare services for the girl child. The initial aim of the campaign was to address the declining Child Sex Ratio (CSR) but has come to include gender-biased sex-selective eliminations, and propagating education, survival, and protection of the girl child.

2. **Sukanya Samriddhi Yojana** Falling under the ambit of the Beti Bachao Beti Padhao scheme, the Sukanya Samriddhi Yojana is a government-backed savings scheme for girl children. The account can be opened at any India Post office or a branch of an authorised commercial bank anytime between the birth of the girl child and till the age of 10 by a parent or guardian.

   (Only one account is allowed per child and parents with a minimum of Rs 1,000 deposited into it. There is no limit to the number of deposits either in a month or in a financial year. The account offers an interest of 8.6 percent.)

3. **Mahila Shakti Kendra The government launched the Mahila Shakti Kendra in 2017** to empower rural women with opportunities for skill development, employment, digital literacy, health and nutrition. The Mahila Shakti Kendras will work through community engagement through student volunteers in the 115 most backward districts. Each Mahila Shakti Kendra will provide an interface for rural women to approach the government to avail of their entitlements through training and capacity building

4. **Mahila-E-Haat Under the purview of the Ministry of Women and Child Development,** the government launched Mahila-E-Haat in 2016. It is a bilingual online marketing platform that leverages technology to help aspiring women entrepreneurs, self-help groups, and NGOs to showcase their products and service.

5. **Working Women Hostel** The government launched the Working Women Hostels to ensure availability of safe, convenient accommodation for working family, along with daycare facilities for their children, wherever possible in urban, semi-urban and rural areas. Under the scheme, assistance is provided for construction of new hostels and expansion of existing ones. The working women hostels are available to any woman provided her gross income does not exceed Rs 50,000 per month in metropolitan cities and Rs 35,000 per month in any other place.

6. **Support to Training and Employment Programme for Women (STEP)** The STEP scheme was set up to provide skills to women so that they can take up gainful employment. It also provides the right competencies and training for women to become entrepreneurs. Open to every woman above the age of 16, it is run through a grant given to an institution/ organisation including NGOs directly. According to the Ministry website, the assistance under STEP Scheme will be available in any sector for imparting skills related to employability and entrepreneurship, including but not limited to the agriculture, horticulture, food processing, handlooms, tailoring, stitching, embroidery, zari, handicrafts, computers & IT-enabled services along with soft skills and skills for the workplace, such as spoken English, gems and jewellery, travel and tourism, and hospitality

Women Empowerment Schemes launch in india.

1. Beti Bachao Beti Padhao Scheme
2. One Stop Centre Scheme
3. Women Helpline Scheme
4. UJJAWALA : A Comprehensive Scheme for Prevention of trafficking and Rescue, Rehabilitation and Re-

integration of Victims of Trafficking and Commercial Sexual Exploitation

5. Working Women Hostel
6. Ministry approves new projects under Ujjawala Scheme and continues existing projects
7. SWADHAR Greh (A Scheme for Women in Difficult Circumstances)
8. NARI SHAKTI PURASKAR
9. Awardees of Stree Shakti Puruskar, 2014 & Awardees of Nari Shakti Puruskar
10. Awardees of Rajya Mahila Samman & Zila Mahila Samman
11. Mahila police Volunteers
12. Mahila Shakti Kendras (MSK)
13. NIRBHAYA

Problem or limitation in India

1. **sexual harassment**
2. **mentally harassment**
3. **domestic violence**
4. **Male dominate society in India . every women feel we are women .these are male.**
5. **Acid throughing**
6. **child marriage**
7. Every year women's day is celebrated on 8th march with a lot of enthusiasm. But Presentally working lady feel every time mentally torcher. women have to free for job but men are not supporting at home because men will be men.

An Indian Wife Is Expected To 'Support', But The Husband Gives Her 'Permission'. Why?

Say it loud and clear, ladies, that what you need from your spouse is a partnership in making family decisions, and support in your personal decisions – not "permission".

8. While interacting with people, one thing that I often come across is, most *men* think they are good husbands if they have 'given permission' to their wives for everything they have asked for. Similarly, most *women* think their husbands are good if the husbands have always permitted them to do what they wanted to do.

9. I have often asked these men if their wives have also given them permission whenever they wanted to do something, and I get a look of **bewildered astonishment**. I have asked women if they too give permission to their husbands whenever they ask for it, and they look shocked, an The difference between permission and support is massive. It's interesting to see how these two are used in accordance to the gender. A woman agreeing with her husband's decisions is "supporting" him while a man agreeing with his wife's decisions is "permitting" her.

10. Things in our society are skewed. Especially in context to **gender roles** and freedom.

11. Questions about our own identity, existence, and about the most basic rights need to be asked. By ourselves to ourselves. No one can give women 'permission' to live their lives their way. Women just have to realise that and BANG! Men would be 'supporting' instead of 'permitting'.

We talk about equality, we talk about not limiting a woman's identity to the gender roles assigned to her by the society but all that talk, and all these ideas go in vain if we dont know how to assert ourselves. And that includes saying

words like "No" and "This is not what I want" loud and clear.

11. Gender inequality is **enmeshed in our social fabric**. A husband cooking for the wife is a good husband but a wife cooking for her husband is well, a wife! A father cleaning up the poop of the child is a good father while a mother doing the same is just a mother! A daughter in law covering her head as a mark of respect is being a daughter in law and a man wishing his in laws is all the respect they need!

12. When gender roles and gender bias happen, they give complete comfort to one side while giving the burden of responsibilities and respect and duties to the other. This means, one side is so comfortable that they would probably not inherently realise that something is skewed in this balance. Thus, expecting the other gender to support is again confirming to the stereotype of looking for approval and permissions. The only way to do it is, doing things not because someone agrees with it or someone supports it or someone is okay with it, but because this is how we look at ourselves and this is how things are going to be!

13. **It is said that change is the rule of the world and with time there have been changes in the role of women.**

Taking care of the house - his feet crossed the threshold and now he has the responsibility of taking care of the house as well as outside.

Home, children and her career outside, everything she is handling. the most prominent challenge to coordinate with home and career. As such, the option of Kamwali (or helping hand) is mostly open to help working women.

And they also adopt her, but even then they also have many such responsibilities which they cannot share

For example, cooking, especially for children, take care of the medicine of the elderly, do the homework of the children. Give them time or take care of children. These are just some of the tasks that she cannot give up on anyone else.

Apart from that, whether it is a job or business, there are a lot of tasks related to it.ex prepare of presentation ,prepare of lecture ,talk to authorities etc There are countless tasks such as trying to complete tasks on time.

Whom she completes. It is not easy to maintain coordination between them. Health is one of the major problems related to working women.

The thing that compromises most when handling home and work.

That is health. She does not eat properly.

Sleep late at night or get up early in the morning. Diseases like headache, body pain, migraine, insomnia become permanent. ladies are taking pain killer but this is not solution they also invite many diseases. she fight every time .

CONCLUSION

Now a day's women workers are improved and promote in their workplace and in technological work. Trade Union should try to improve the conditions for woman's workers in many parts for example maternity leave is easily give to women and help the woman for achieve higher post actually women's nature is promotion to gain high quality in every field but if the condition is not ready then the reduction of promotion and optimization in work will be occur and etc...

Women workers are often subject to sexual harassment then the Government should put strict rules for these types of crimes , also public transport system sometimes danger for woman and Government should put more Inspection. Traditionally people think that men should only work and ga are increasing that's why women also should company in gaining income for families. Therefore a fundamental change is required in attitudes of employees, family members and public.in money and women should work as house hold, but The financial demands on the Indian families.

Now a days men thinking or attitude. these person should be take all responsibility for family not only job. women also human being not a machine so ladies also want to relaxation in life. we think ladies suffer in life every time.

> *Woman is an incarnation of 'Shakti' – the Goddess of Power. If she is bestowed with education, India's strength will double. Let the campaign of 'Kanya Kelavni' be spread in every home; let the lamp of educating daughters be lit up in every heart*
>
> *– Narendra Modi*

References

- Dashora, (2013) Problems Faced by Working Women in India.*International Journal of Advanced Research in Management and Social Sciences*, 2(8), PP (82-94).
- Aditi, M. (1997).feminist organizing in India, a study of women in NGOs. *Aditi-Mitra- Feminist-Organizing-In-India-A-Study-Of-Women-In-Ngos.*
- Kumari,V. *(2014)*.Problems and Challenges Faced by Urban Worming Women in India. *A Dissertation Submitted to the Department of Humanities and Social Sciences, (1)*
- Kumar, P. &Sundar, K. (2012). Problems Faced by Women Executives Working in Public Sector Banks in Puducherry.*International Journal of Marketing, Financial Services & Management Research.*1(7), PP 180-193.
- Karl, M. (2009).Inseparable: The Crucial Role of Women in Food Security Revisited. Women in Action. No.1, 2009, PP 8-19.
- Murthy, G. K. (2012).Women and Corporate Leadership- in Indian Perspectives.*IRACSTInternational Journal of Research in Management & Technology.*2(4) PP 377-382.